Sacrifice

The Essence of Life

John W. Abell

WESTBOW
PRESS
A DIVISION OF THOMAS NELSON

WestBow Press books may be ordered through booksellers or by contacting:

WestBow Press
A Division of Thomas Nelson
1663 Liberty Drive
Bloomington, IN 47403
www.westbowpress.com
1-(866) 928-1240

ISBN: 978-1-4497-8992-3 (sc)
ISBN: 978-1-4497-8993-0 (hc)
ISBN: 978-1-4497-8991-6 (e)

Library of Congress Control Number: 2013906388

Printed in the United States of America.

WestBow Press rev. date: 05/23/2013

This book is dedicated to the brave men and women who have risked and given their lives in the service of their country and for the principles, ideals, and quest for human dignity and freedom on which these United States were founded. In the annals of United States history, the sacrifice of untold thousands of American lives to the cause of human freedom and dignity in this country and throughout the world cannot be overstated. Without their commitment, devotion, inspiration, and example, our great country and our unparalleled freedoms would not exist today.

Table of Contents

List of Illustrations

Introduction

Five, four, three, two … the shot goes up … one. The ball hits the backboard, catches the rim, and just misses as the horn ends the final game of the 2010 NCAA Men's Basketball Finals. Duke 71, Butler 69. Gordon Hayward, Butler's amazing sophomore guard sensation, just missed his last-second desperation shot from half court. Had the shot gone in, Butler would have been the NCAA Men's 2010 Basketball champions. What a story!

Butler? Who was Butler, and how did they get to the final game of the NCAA basketball tournament in 2010? I'm sure there were thousands, probably millions, across the country and the world who had never heard of Butler University. But now I would bet there are thousands, maybe millions more, who do know about Butler. Why? Because this same small private school located on the north side of Indianapolis did the unimaginable, the unthinkable. Butler repeated the miracle of 2010 in 2011. The Butler Bulldogs made another run at the national title by defeating the likes of Pitt and Florida in the 2011 NCAA tournament run that put them right back in the final game of the NCAA tournament for a second consecutive year. Although the Bulldogs fell to Connecticut in that game, there was no doubt about it—the Bulldogs were for real!

I am a 1972 graduate of Butler University and proud of it. Over the years, I've followed the "Dawgs" closely and attended many games at Hinkle Fieldhouse, the iconic basketball treasure built in 1927 that still has the hallowed look of a true basketball arena. Most know the Indiana high school basketball state final's scenes in the famed movie *Hoosiers* were filmed at Hinkle Fieldhouse. Even commentators on ESPN and CBS make comments about how walking into Hinkle Fieldhouse is like walking into the past, giving a unique perspective of the history of college basketball.

And yes, I was at Lucas Oil Stadium in April 2010 when Butler beat Michigan State in the NCAA semifinal and lost to Duke in the final game. Like most everyone else, I have been amazed at the rise of Butler basketball over the past decade, culminating in two successive NCAA final appearances. But the real question is not who or where Butler is but rather, how did this small private school of four thousand students get to the final game of the NCAA tournament, not just once but two years in a row? That is a feat that is difficult for even the most dominant basketball schools like Duke, North Carolina, Kansas, and Kentucky—the thoroughbreds of college hoops.

I would not presume to know all the ins and outs of what makes Butler basketball the great program it has become. However, there are those who would like to explain it away as "just lucky" or that Butler had easy routes through the tournament. But for those who make such extemporaneous (and ridiculous, I might add) comments, it is obvious they have not done their homework. There are a multitude of reasons Butler accomplished what it did in 2010 and 2011. But I'm sure the coaches and players would all use a similar term defining the one reason Butler's teams accomplished what seemed to be the impossible: sacrifice.

We often use, and probably overuse, the word *sacrifice* without thought of its true meaning. After all, sacrifice occurs in a variety of ways and in varying degrees every single day. We all sacrifice, right? You can find various definitions for the word, but whatever definition you find, it usually comes down to a single concept: to give up something of value for the benefit of another.

So did Butler's basketball coaches and players sacrifice more than all the other NCAA coaches and teams (except Duke and Connecticut)? Of course not. Who could begin to measure the amount of sacrifice? Coach Stevens worked harder than all the other coaches in the Horizon League, right? He worked harder than Florida's Billy Donovan, right? Brad Stevens worked harder than Pitt's Jamie Dixon, right? And the Butler players worked harder too, right? I think you get my point—most coaches and players work their tails off through the season and into the tournament. Thousands of hours of preparation on and off the court are part of nearly all NCAA basketball programs. Thousands of hours of workouts, film-room sessions, drills, and repetitions that would bore most people to death are just part of the package. Yes, Butler's coaches and players did sacrifice—as much, maybe even more, than their opponents. But sacrifice isn't about comparisons. Sacrifice is about the act itself, to give up something of value for the benefit of another.

The concept of sacrifice is as old as the human race. It applies in all areas of life, not just in the arena of athletics. All people have, at specific times in their lives to a greater or lesser degree, performed sacrificial acts. My general purpose in writing this book is to look at a variety of human actions that can be defined as sacrificial to gain a greater appreciation for those who, throughout their lives, directly or indirectly, and even in ways unrelated to our personal lives have sacrificed in ways that have benefited our culture, our society, and most importantly, our world. In our secular, relativist, and pragmatic world, where so many appear to be myopic and "me focused," I hope those who read this book will take a fresh look at their own lives, realizing the blessings they experience every single day have been bought with a price—the price of sacrifice.

In the closing lines of a speech delivered in Los Angeles in 1964, future US president Ronald Reagan said,

> You and I know and do not believe that life is so dear and peace so sweet as to be purchased at the price of chains and slavery. If nothing in life is worth dying for, when did this begin—just in the face of this enemy? Or should Moses have told the children of Israel to live in slavery under the pharaohs? Should Christ have refused the cross? Should the patriots at Concord Bridge have thrown down their guns and refused to fire the shot heard 'round the world? The martyrs of history were not fools, and our honored dead who gave their lives to stop the advance of the Nazis didn't die in vain. Where, then, is the road to peace? Well it's a simple answer after all. You and I have the courage to say to our enemies, "There is a price we will not pay. There is a point beyond which they must not advance." Winston Churchill said, "The destiny of man is not measured by material computations. When great forces are on the move in the world, we learn we're spirits—not animals." And he said, "There's something going on in time and space, and beyond time and space, which, whether we like it or not, spells duty." You and I have a rendezvous with destiny. We'll preserve for our children this, the last best hope of man on earth, or we'll sentence

them to take the last step into a thousand years of darkness.[1]

One might conclude after reading the first three chapters of this work that this book glorifies war. But nothing could be further from the truth. Whether the reader would agree or not, humanity is and always has been at war—a spiritual war between good and evil that often throughout the pages of human history has manifested itself on the battlefields of human warfare. But this book is not all about war as we perceive it. This book is about heroes—American heroes, heroes of humanity, and most importantly, heroes of faith. And this work is about appreciating, respecting, and being thankful for the unselfish sacrifices made by heroes who throughout this world's history have risked and given their lives for causes that are good—justice, freedom, and individual rights—causes that God fully ordains and supports in his holy Word.

While reading about the sacrifices mentioned in the pages of this book, my hope as the author is that each reader will look introspectively and determine how personal sacrifice is possible, not only in the large scope of the human experience to which President Reagan's speech alluded but personally, within the realm of the reader's daily living. Like it or not, we all have a duty as American citizens and as humans. What can each person do every day to give up something of value, however great or small, for the benefit of another person or group of persons? Personal sacrifice can be any action from the most miniscule contribution to a large humanitarian effort. But the key and the ultimate result of a sacrificial action must be to benefit others.

Many of the true stories found in *Sacrifice: The Essence of Life* are of men and women who made the ultimate sacrifice—the giving of their lives. Obviously, that act is the most extreme form of sacrifice. Hopefully, those who read this book will not be called upon to make that kind of sacrifice. But what if you were? Could you do it? Although the odds are small that each of us will be called to make the ultimate sacrifice, all of us are called upon daily to make some form of sacrifice. Are you ready and prepared to make these sacrifices, however great or small? The stories that follow will inspire you and hopefully make you more determined to make the sacrifices that you will confront in your own daily life.

Finally, my specific purpose in writing *Sacrifice* is twofold: 1) to remember that historical sacrifices have been made that have given us the blessings of freedom and life that we enjoy each and every day; and 2) to support orphans in South Africa. All profits from the sale of this book will support Horizon International, a nonprofit Christian relief and development organization whose purpose is to minister to orphaned children whose lives have been negatively affected by HIV/AIDS. According to Horizon International's mission, children are served regardless of race, gender, or religion with the purpose of breaking the cycle of poverty and disease that so often entraps them. Visit the Horizon International website at www. horizoninternationalinc.org.

We would all do well to follow the godly wisdom and direction found in James 1:27, which says, "Religion that God our Father accepts as pure and faultless is this: to look after orphans and widows in their distress and to keep oneself from being polluted by the world" (New International Version).

Chapter 1

A Time Nearly Forgotten

The day was warm and sunny, with some clouds casting distinct shadows over the harbor. The waters of Pearl Harbor were clear blue. Unlike the chaos and devastation of December 7, 1941, this day was calm, quiet, and beautiful. Standing on the deck of the USS *Missouri*, I was about to participate in one of the most moving experiences of my life. The date was Saturday, November 24, 2007. I had been offered the privilege and honor of raising the flag of the United States of America in the morning flag ceremony on the Battleship *Missouri*, which was anchored in Pearl Harbor not more than two hundred yards from the USS *Arizona* Memorial. The band began to play the *National Anthem*. As I began pulling the rope to hoist "Old Glory" to its zenith overlooking the ship, tears started falling from my eyes. As I listened to the *National Anthem*, which I had heard probably a thousand times before, I became very emotional. I was on the deck of the ship where the Japanese surrender had occurred in Tokyo Bay on September 2, 1945. I was standing in almost the exact location where the Japanese delegation had signed the Formal Instrument of Surrender in the presence of General Douglas MacArthur, supreme allied commander, bringing a close to the most deadly war in the history of civilization. The Japanese delegation onboard the *Missouri* that September day represented the country that had planned and perpetrated the dastardly attack on Pearl Harbor, taking the lives of 2,395 Americans and wounding or injuring thousands more. As I looked out across the bow of the huge battleship just a few hundred yards away, I could see the *Arizona* Memorial.

View of USS *Arizona* Memorial at flag raising ceremony, November 24, 2007.

It was such a humbling and reverent moment. I still have the flag. It was given to me as a gift. Later, as we walked onto the *Arizona* Memorial and I looked down into the water to see the rusting hulk of the USS *Arizona*, perhaps for the first time in my adult life the thought of real human sacrifice hit me square in the face. Directly below lay the remains of more than eleven hundred US navy men who sacrificed their lives doing their duty and serving their country in the cause of human freedom around the world. Then a more staggering thought took hold of me—more than four hundred thousand Americans sacrificed their lives from 1941-45. As time passed and my inspiration grew, my thoughts about sacrifice expanded even further. What about the whole of American history? Sacrifices were made throughout our country's history—not just during World War II. I knew then that if I wrote about American sacrifices, it would be only exemplary. There has been no book ever written that encompasses the complete spectrum of American sacrifice proclaiming all American lives lost in the quest for human freedom and in the service of their country. And, in my humble opinion, no book can ever be written that can accomplish that monumental task. However, I can honestly say as I reflect on my visit to Pearl Harbor on November 24, 2007, "I will never forget that day!"

In the fall of 2007, while serving as assistant principal at Carmel High School, Carmel, Indiana, my wife and I had been invited to accompany the marching band on a unique trip to Hawaii. The band had two performances and an invitation to play at the daily opening ceremonies on board the USS *Missouri*. I am not sure how it happened, but I was asked to do the flag raising ceremony. Shortly after the ceremony we visited the USS *Arizona* Memorial. A wonderful man named Allen Bodenlos, a Pearl Harbor survivor, was our guide and chaperone. He was an amazing man, about eighty-five years old. He was a walking history book. Allen arrived at Pearl Harbor on December 6, 1941—one day before the attack.

**John and Gloria with Pearl Harbor survivor Allen Bodenlos—
November 24, 2007—Pearl Harbor, Hawaii.**

The entire Pearl Harbor experience was staggering, standing on the memorial looking down, and with no difficulty, seeing the large hulk of the *Arizona* below. After looking at the white "wall of remembrance" inside the memorial, where the list of the names of those who perished on December 7, 1941, seemed almost endless, and then walking only a few steps and looking down at the ship where 1,102 men were entombed, having sacrificed their lives—it moved me in such a solemn way—I thought about the price of freedom. As I watched beads of oil, still coming to the surface from the sunken vessel after more than sixty-five years, I thought mostly of what sacrifice was all about and how blessed I was because of the sacrifices made by those who lay in that watery grave.

Most of us do not take the time, or circumstances do not prompt us, to think about our freedoms or our blessings, and perhaps most importantly, the staggering cost of those freedoms and blessings. I recently viewed the lengthy series *The Pacific* produced by Steven

Spielberg. The DVD series contains about eight DVDs recounting the Pacific War during the years 1942-45. I have been a student of history most of my life. My undergraduate degree major was US history. I taught US history and related subjects for ten years at Carmel High School in Carmel, Indiana, before assuming responsibilities as a high school administrator at that same school. I have read a little history in my lifetime. Actually, I have read a lot of history. But as much as I have read and continue to read, there is something about actual video from historical events or, as in Spielberg's *The Pacific*, a well-directed and well-acted version of history based on fact, not Hollywood fiction, that cuts to one's heart lying open a host of feelings and emotions about the events depicted. The one thing about Spielberg's account of the Pacific War that separates it from war documentary footage is that Spielberg personalizes his film account of the Pacific campaign. The viewer sees the story of real people as those people experienced it and recorded it.

The research done for *The Pacific* came through a painstaking records review and most importantly, through the interviews of those gallant men who survived Guadalcanal, Peleliu, Iwo Jima, and Okinawa. Most of the movie comes from the personal memoirs of Robert Leckie and Eugene Sledge. Private Leckie served in How Company, Second Battalion of the First Marine Division in the Pacific theatre. After Pearl Harbor he enlisted in the Marine Corps and served as a machine gunner participating in every major campaign except Okinawa. He was wounded by a shell blast on the island of Peleliu, ending his combat experience. Leckie said he had a story to tell of what the war was really like. He wrote his first and best-selling book, *Helmet for My Pillow*, which was his personal memoir, published in 1957. But Leckie didn't stop there. He wrote many books on several American wars. Leckie died in 2001.

Eugene Sledge volunteered for the Marine Corps in December 1942, six months after graduating high school. He was assigned to King Company, Third Battalion, Fifth Marines, First Marine Division. He served in the Pacific Theatre and was in combat as a mortar man at Peleliu and Okinawa. Private Sledge kept copious notes on what happened during battle. Interestingly, he kept his notes in his pocket New Testament. After serving a short stint in China after the war, he was discharged in 1946. Sledge went on to graduate from Alabama Polytechnic Institute in 1949. In the years following, he transferred his notes into a personal memoir known as *With the Old Breed*. The book was first published in 1981.

Understand that Sledge and Leckie are just two men representing a total of nearly sixteen million men and women who served during World War II. Of that sixteen million, more than four hundred thousand perished. As I watched the episodes of *The Pacific*, I was spellbound at the thought of having to endure such squalid and appalling conditions not even considering the fact that while enduring those horrid conditions, they were fighting a life-and-death battle with a merciless enemy. Sledge and Leckie represent thousands of soldiers who sacrificed on a daily basis in the Pacific campaign. Their lives in hell during those months are far beyond our ability to comprehend.

Another heroic and sacrificial story is that of John Basilone, also known as the hero of Guadalcanal. Private Basilone's story is well documented. The following account is reported on the website Marines in World War II, vividly explaining what John Basilone did on Sunday night, October 25, 1942. The following is just a snapshot account. Further research will astound you regarding the bravery and heroism that occurred on Guadalcanal.

"About midnight, from the gloom of ink-black darkness came hundreds of screaming Japanese troops. Throwing themselves on the flesh-cutting barbed wire, the first of the waves formed human bridges for their comrades to leap across. One of the Marine section leaders facing them was Sergeant John 'Manila' Basilone. An experienced machine gunner, Basilone knew his guns would be tested to their mechanical limits. It would be up to him to keep them firing. During the attack, when grenades, small arms, and machine guns were ripping the night and exploding human flesh splattered friend and foe, Sergeant Basilone stayed with his malaria-ridden men. Repeatedly repairing guns and changing barrels in almost total darkness, he ran for ammo or steadied his terrified men, who were firing full trigger to keep a sheet of white-hot lead pouring into the ranks of the charging Japanese. Bodies piled so high in front of his weapons pits they had to be reset so the barrels could fire over the piles of corpses. Not even the famous water-cooled heavy machine guns could stop all the assaults, and one section of guns was overrun. Two men killed, three others wounded. When he received the nation's highest decoration, John Basilone replied modestly, 'Only part of this medal belongs to me. Pieces of it belong to the boys who are still on Guadalcanal. It was rough as hell down there.'"[1] Gunnery Sergeant John Basilone voluntarily returned to the Pacific War. He was sent to the sands of Iwo Jima February 19, 1945, to lead another machine gun squad. Iwo Jima would be his toughest fight. Barely on the island two hours, he was killed leading his men. Gunnery Sergeant John "Manila" Basilone was the only marine in WWII to receive both the Medal of Honor and the Navy Cross.

To recount the dreadful conditions that existed on the islands of the Pacific or on the battlefields of Europe or the prisoner of war camps that were found in every theater of that horrendous war would be too extensive a task for the purpose of this writing. Those accounts have already been written, as I have alluded to with Sledge, Leckie's, and hundreds of other historical and personal writings.

Remember my theme—sacrifice. To give one pertinent example— Iwo Jima. The battle for the island of Iwo Jima was actually near the end of the war. The battle lasted thirty-six days. February 19-March 26, 1945. But it was one of the bloodiest campaigns of the war. During the entire four years of the Pacific War, nineteen thousand Marines were killed. During the thirty-six days of Iwo Jima, six thousand Marines met their death. More than eighteen thousand more were injured in battle. Of the six soldiers who hoisted the American flag on Mount Suribachi, three didn't live to see the end of the battle.[2]

The battle for Okinawa, an island chain considered part of Japan, was a similar story. The battle lasted nearly three months. The total US killed numbered more than twelve thousand. Another forty thousand were wounded. Of the 117,000 Japanese defending Okinawa, approximately 110,000 were killed.[3]

Sacrifice in World War II's Pacific theatre—the list is endless. Guadalcanal, Midway, Peleliu, the Solomon Islands, Tarawa, Iwo Jima, Okinawa, and innumerable other locations where brave, frightened young soldiers put their lives on the line. Not just momentarily but for days, weeks, and months on end. Men—young men—who had a duty, committed themselves to that duty and did it. These were men who put their lives on the line for their fellow soldiers, for their families, for their country, and for their belief in fighting for the freedom of enslaved people on the other side of the world.

The conditions were unbelievably hellish: swamps, snakes, mosquitoes, malaria, squalid conditions, lack of food and water, and worst of all, an enemy that was unscrupulous and inhumane. "Japan's military-dominated government had long been preparing for its quest for world power. Over decades, it had crafted a muscular, technologically sophisticated army and navy, and through a military-run school system that relentlessly and violently drilled children on the nation's imperial destiny, for decades it had shaped its people for war. Finally, through intense indoctrination, beatings, and desensitization, its army cultivated and celebrated extreme brutality in its soldiers."[4]

Historian Iris Chang wrote about the Japanese military machine, saying, "Imbuing violence with holy meaning, the Japanese imperial army made violence a cultural imperative every bit as powerful as that which propelled Europeans during the Crusades and the Spanish Inquisition."[5]

For those Allied soldiers who served in the Pacific theater, without question their greatest fear was being captured by the Japanese. With the perspective of cultural superiority indoctrinated into every Japanese soldier's mind, as well as the tendency toward violence and cruelty toward all enemies, the reputation of the Japanese army was basically that of a murderous horde.

Although there are a multitude of examples of the brutality of the Japanese military, perhaps the best example occurred in 1937, years before Americans were fighting the Japanese in the Pacific. Japan invaded Manchuria in 1931. But in 1937 the Japanese army surrounded the Chinese city of Nanking. Inside the city were nearly five hundred thousand Chinese civilians, as well as almost one hundred thousand Chinese soldiers. The Chinese soldiers surrendered with the promise of being treated well. Once in a POW camp and mostly bound, the Japanese military high command issued orders to execute all Chinese military personnel. "What followed was a six-week frenzy of killing that defies articulation. Masses of POWs were beheaded, machine-gunned, bayoneted, and burned alive. The Japanese turned on civilians, engaging in killing contests, raping tens of thousands of Chinese women, mutilating and crucifying them, and provoking dogs to maul them. Historians estimate that the Japanese military murdered between two hundred thousand and four hundred thirty thousand Chinese, including ninety thousand POWs, in what has become known as the Rape of Nanking."[6]

During World War II there were millions of US military men and women who risked their lives in the service of their country, and I will mention a few a little later in this chapter. But what about the Germans? Were they all stark-raving Nazis like Adolph Hitler and his criminal gang, who in the "perfect storm" of political, social, and economic unrest seized power in Germany in the early 1930s? Absolutely not!

What about Colonel Claus von Stauffenberg? Who? Do you remember? He was one of the conspirators, or should I say German patriots, who plotted to kill Adolph Hitler in 1944. How did he sacrifice anything? Actually, he sacrificed everything, putting his life, as well as the lives of his wife and five children on the line by planning to kill Hitler and establish a government that would negotiate an end to the war in Europe before Germany was totally destroyed while saving countless lives in the meantime.

Stauffenberg was a principled man who was brought up in the teachings of the Catholic church. His family was prominent in the German aristocracy. Although well-educated, he, like many aristocratic young men following family military regiments, pursued a military career. Stauffenberg saw action in both the Polish and French invasions. However, he was "on the fence," not supporting Hitler's political views and policies (National Socialism) but being drawn to Der Fuhrer's military insights.

By 1942, especially after the failed Russian invasion, it was becoming clear that Germany was heading toward difficult times and most likely an eventual defeat. Stauffenberg was extremely troubled by Hitler's heinous policies toward Jews and political opponents. It was at this time, while serving in North Africa in 1943 that he was severely wounded by British aircraft in a strafing incident. Sent back to Berlin for hospitalization and treatment for the loss of one eye and amputation of his hand, Stauffenberg came in contact with resistance sources within the German military, as well as other Germans with some measure of influence and resources. Colonel Claus von Stauffenberg, after his recuperation and rehabilitation, was appointed the Chief of Staff of the Reserve Army designed to protect Berlin and Adolph Hitler in a crisis situation. Colonel von Stauffenberg saw the urgency of the situation and what was going to happen to Germany if Hitler was not taken out of power. The only way that could happen was for Hitler to be assassinated. He made the choice not only to become part of the conspiracy, but in the ultra highly secured environment in which Hitler operated, he was one of very few officers who had the opportunity to carry out such a plot. The chance of success was extremely small, but von Stauffenberg knew what hung in the balance—the fate of his family, Germany, and perhaps the world.

You probably know the story. In abbreviated form, Colonel von Stauffenberg plotted to carry a small but deadly explosive into the "wolf's lair"—Hitler's military planning compound in East Prussia.

His purpose was to plant the bomb (hidden in his briefcase), exit the planning room under pretense of a phone call, and be within safe distance of the bunker when the explosive detonated. He would then fly back to Berlin to put in place a military plan known as "Valkyrie," taking control of the government under a crisis situation (Hitler's assassination).

The bomb did explode, but Hitler was not killed—only shaken, with an injury to his hand. Others in the bunker were killed or more seriously wounded, but Hitler survived. Needless to say, things went downhill from there and eventually, over the course of several hours, von Stauffenberg and his cadre of conspirators were rounded up and summarily executed. Von Stauffenberg was taken immediately to the courtyard of the war ministry building and executed by firing squad.[7]

Miraculously, Stauffenberg's wife and children remained safe. His wife, Nina, died of natural causes in Germany in 2006. Again, sacrifice? Putting everything on the line under potentially violent and life-threatening consequences. We must realize that this is one of many such stories in the lives of countless Germans fighting in the resistance against Hitler. Sacrifices were made daily … lives were sacrificed daily in the attempt to redeem Germany and overcome the evil, violent, murderous plague of Nazism.

On the memorial to the German Resistance located near the spot of his execution in Berlin, Stauffenberg and other resistance fighters are memorialized with these words: "Ihr trugt die Schande nicht. Ihr wehrtet euch. Ihr gabt das Grobe ewig wache Zeichen der Umkehr, opfernde Euer heibses Leben fur Freiheit, Recht, und Ehre." This translates, "You did not bear the shame. You resisted. You bestowed an eternally vigilant symbol of change by sacrificing your impassioned lives for freedom, justice, and honor."

Dietrich Bonhoeffer was another German patriot. Who was he? Pastor Dietrich Bonhoeffer was a renowned German scholar, pastor, and teacher who became a known force in the German resistance movement. Bonhoeffer went so far in his efforts to save Germany from sure destruction that he, acting in the capacity of an agent or spy, attempted to make contact with the British on behalf of the German resistance. Bonhoeffer was found out and executed by the Nazis on April 9, 1945, less than one month from the war's end.[8] Perhaps Bonhoeffer said it best: "Who stands firm? Only the one whose final standard is not his reason, his principles, his conscience, his freedom, his virtue, but who is ready to sacrifice all these, when in faith and sole allegiance to God he is called to obedient and responsible action: the responsible person, whose life will be nothing but an answer to God's question and call."[9]

How many of us have read or seen *Schindler's List*? Oskar Schindler, the hero, right? Oskar Schindler, the man who saved more than twelve hundred Jews from the gas chambers, right? Yes, that's him. But it is ironic that this non-military World War II hero was actually a very rich man who lost his fortune, joined the Nazi party because he was bankrupt, and was on his way to remaking his fortune at the expense of free Jewish labor working at a factory he acquired through bribes during the war years. Schindler came from a wealthy family who lost their fortune in the Depression years of the 1930s. But Oskar Schindler became a war profiteer, making millions on the forced labor of Jews under the Nazi regime.

But you know the story. Schindler changed. It's never too late to change! He finally realized the ultimate horror of the Nazis' "final solution" and decided to do something about it. He took Jews who were destined to death camps and transferred them to his factory, where, through the manipulation of his books, hundreds of Jews who otherwise would have perished in the camps were given food, medicine, and protection. Schindler did this knowing that if he were found out, it would be his life that the Nazis would likely take.

After the war, having spent his fortune assisting the Jews, Schindler moved to South America but later returned to Germany in the late 1950s. He was hated and persecuted in Germany because of his reminder of the war years for those who did nothing to prevent the Holocaust. Schindler died in Germany in 1974 but was buried in Jerusalem at his own request. Acts of extreme sacrifice are usually accompanied by extreme risks. Oskar Schindler risked and sacrificed his fortune to save hundreds of Jewish lives. Schindler also risked his very life in the process and died an outcast in his own country.[10]

What about American sacrifice? It would take volumes to name them all. But I can give a few examples. In the words of President Franklin D. Roosevelt, the Pearl Harbor attack of December 7, 1941, was a "date that will live in infamy." Cook Third Class, Doris "Dorie" Miller, was a black mess attendant shipman serving on the USS *West Virginia* on December 7, 1941. He was the heavyweight boxing champion of his ship. Although a mess attendant (only because race still played a major role in military assignments) when the Japanese attack commenced, he continually carried the wounded to safety. He subsequently came to the aid of the mortally wounded captain of the USS *West Virginia* and then manned a .50 caliber machine gun until the order came to abandon the sinking ship. The Japanese surprise attack lasted fewer than two hours but long enough to result in staggering casualties. A total of 2,395 Americans were killed. and 1,143 were wounded. After the "date that will live in infamy," Dorie Miller continued to serve in the Pacific theatre throughout the war, being assigned to various ships and duties. However, during the siege of the Gilbert Islands in November 1943, Miller was serving on the USS *Liscome Bay*. That ship was torpedoed and the ship's bomb magazine exploded. Among the ship's missing was Dorie Miller. Miller put himself in harm's way at Pearl Harbor, rescuing fellow sailors and manning the antiaircraft gun. He continued his service, placing himself in harm's way in the Pacific theatre of war, dying in the service of his country for the sake of freedom at home and abroad.[11]

There are thousands of stories that followed the survivors of Pearl Harbor, and 2,395 stories of sacrifice ended that dreadful Sunday, December 7, 1941.

Most of us who have even a passing interest and knowledge of World War II know about D-Day. Many of us viewed in horror the realistic D-Day landing scenes in the movie *Saving Private Ryan*. D-Day was the largest amphibious invasion in world history and was executed by land, sea, and air forces under direct British command, with more than 160,000 troops landing on June 6, 1944. The combined Allied naval, air, and land forces numbered approximately 195,700.

Part of the Sixteenth Infantry Regiment of the D-Day landings, Tech Sergeant John J. Pinder Jr. was wounded twice and refused medical attention in order to establish radio communications on the Normandy beaches. When he landed near the beach, he was a hundred yards offshore. Under horrendous fire from German machine gunners and artillery and weakened by loss of blood due to his wounds, Tech Sergeant Pinder, not once, not twice, but three times entered the water to retrieve communications equipment that was necessary to establishing the radio link vital to success on the beach under enemy fire. Continuing his attempts to gather equipment and establish communication on the Normandy beach, Pinder was wounded a third time, which proved fatal. He died on his thirty-second birthday. He was posthumously awarded the Congressional Medal of Honor, the nation's highest honor for bravery, seven months later. His Medal of Honor citation reads, "For conspicuous gallantry and intrepidity above and beyond the call of duty on 6 June, 1944, near Colleville-sur-Mer, France." John J. Pinder is buried in Grandview Cemetery in Florence, Pennsylvania.[12]

On April 24, 1997, the *New York Times* printed an article stating that Henry Mucci had died at the age of eighty-eight. The article remembered him as the leader of a group of commandos who rescued five hundred survivors of the Bataan Death March from a Japanese POW camp in the Philippines. The article said, "Henry A. Mucci, the charismatic army colonel who became an instant and enduring American war hero in 1945 when he led the raid that rescued five hundred survivors of the fall of Corregidor and the Bataa Death March from a Japanese prison camp in the Philippines, died on Sunday at a hospital near his home in Melbourne, Fla. He was eighty-eight."

Lt. Colonel Henry Mucci, in the final months of World War II, led a ranger unit consisting of 128 army rangers and approximately 250 Filipino guerillas behind Japanese lines to rescue more than 500 POWs from a Japanese concentration camp called Cabanatuan Prison Camp. Most of the prisoners rescued were near death. In the nearly three years of their imprisonment, many POWs died of starvation, malnutrition, or were executed in the camp since the Bataan Death March brought them there in April, 1942.[13]

The mission was more than dangerous; it was a great risk. Going behind enemy lines and attempting to rescue such a large number of POWs who were weak, sick, and dying seemed nearly futile. What did these rangers and Filipino guerillas sacrifice? The risk of the ultimate sacrifice was great. However, due to surprise, good planning, dedication to those who had suffered for so long in the Japanese POW camp, and perhaps even some luck (and, I'm sure, some divine intervention), the raid resulted in the death of only two rangers. They liberated 489 POWs and 33 civilians, from Cabanatuan.

And what about President John F. Kennedy's heroism in the Solomon Islands in 1943? Heroism and sacrifice personified. The PT 109 commanded by Kennedy with executive officer, Ensign Leonard Jay Thom and ten enlisted men, was one of the fifteen boats sent out on patrol on the night of August 1, 1943, to intercept Japanese warships in the straits. A friend of Kennedy, Ensign George H. R. Ross, whose ship was damaged, joined Kennedy's crew that night. The PT boat was creeping along to keep the wake and noise to a minimum in order to avoid detection.

Around 0200 hours, with Kennedy at the helm, the Japanese destroyer Amagiri, traveling at forty knots, cut PT 109 in half in less than ten seconds. Although the Japanese destroyer had not realized that their ship had struck an enemy vessel, the damage to PT 109 was severe. At impact, Kennedy was thrown into the cockpit, where he landed on his bad back.

As Amagiri steamed away, its wake doused the flames on the floating section of PT 109, to which five Americans clung. Kennedy yelled out for others in the water and heard the replies of Ross and five members of the crew, two of which were injured. Charles A. Harris had an injured leg and Patrick Henry McMahon, the engineer was badly burned. Kennedy swam to these men, and although they were only one hundred yards from the floating piece of the PT 109, in the dark it took Kennedy three hours to tow McMahon and help Harris back to the PT hulk.

Unfortunately, crewmen Andrew Jackson Kirksey and Harold W. Marney were killed in the collision with the Japanese destroyer. Because the remnant was listing badly and starting to swamp, Kennedy decided to swim for a small island barely visible (actually three miles) to the southeast. Five hours later, all eleven survivors had made it to the island after having spent a total of fifteen hours in the water.[14] Kennedy did not have to go back. He did not have to put his own life in jeopardy to save the lives of others. But he did. He risked his own life to save the lives of his comrades.

The year was the same, 1943. The theater of war was the same— the Pacific theater of World War II. But the location is not exact. All he could see in every direction was the dark waters of the Pacific. Louie Zamperini, an Olympic distance runner and boyhood juvenile delinquent, was looking over an expanse of the Pacific Ocean after his B-24 Liberator bomber, whose engines had failed, crashed into the ocean on a search and rescue mission. Only seven years earlier he had shaken the hand of Adolph Hitler. Zamperini had just completed the five thousand meter run in Olympic stadium at the 1936 Berlin Olympics. Shortly after the race Louie went to the Fuhrer's box and asked Joseph Goebbels, Hitler's Minister of Propaganda, if he could snap a picture of Der Fuhrer. Zamperini was escorted into Hitler's box and Adolph Hitler said to him, "Ah, you're the boy with the fast finish."[15] Louie had just run his final lap of the five thousand meter run in a record time of fifty-six seconds.

But now in 1943, somewhere in the Pacific, Zamperini had nearly lost his life in the ocean crash. But what lay ahead was much worse.

Zamperini and two other surviving crewmen drifted for forty-seven days in the endless blue Pacific while traveling the ocean currents for more than two thousand miles. When the Japanese found Zamperini and one crewman (the other crewman died on the raft and was buried at sea), Louie, once weighing about 165 pounds, now weighed 79 pounds.[16]

During captivity, Zamperini was used as a guinea pig by a Japanese doctor and injected with a variety of toxic substances. The experiments stopped only when he blacked out. On the wall of his wooden cell, he later found a crude engraving: "Nine marines marooned on Makin Island—August 12, 1942." The names of the marines followed. It turned out those men had been beheaded. Zamperini memorized the names so he could report their fate on his return home.[17]

Interestingly, at one of the Japanese POW camps, Louie came face to face with someone he remembered from his days at the USC campus. The Japanese interrogator was James Sasaki, who had actually been a Japanese spy in pre-war California. Louie Zamperini remained in Japanese captivity until the end of World War II. After the war, Zamperini found himself somewhat confused and unsure of what to do next. He often thought of the 1948 Olympics in London, but his battered body was just not up to the task of training for competition. Zamperini sank into despair and, once again, turned to alcohol and a brawling lifestyle. It took conversion under the ministry of the Reverend Billy Graham to turn things around. In 1950, Louie Zamperini returned to Japan as a missionary. He sought out many of those who had tortured and tormented him in the POW camps with the sole purpose of telling them they were forgiven. His previous acquaintance, James Sasaki, remained in military prison until 1952. Louie had personally pleaded for Sasaki's acquittal to

General Douglas MacArthur but was unsuccessful. After the whole ordeal, Louie simply stated, "I've been blessed!"[18] At the age of ninety-four, Louie Zamperini currently resides in California and still travels and speaks of his "blessed life."

Along with Louis Zamperini, on an earlier mission over the island of Nauru was a bombardier named Harry Brooks. The island of Nauru was a smallish island, only eight square miles, somewhere about twenty-five hundred miles southwest of Hawaii. The Japanese had seized the island in 1942 and forced the natives, as well as Chinese, to mine the island's most highly valued resource—phosphate. Phosphate was the key ingredient used to make various munitions as well as fertilizer. Obviously, in a world at war, fertilizer and weapons were important products. Louis Zamperini, Harry Brooks, and the crew of the B-24 Liberator, affectionately called *Super Man*, were on a mission to bomb the small island and destroy any of its capacity to produce and mine the precious mineral resource.[19]

However, the Japanese were ready and waiting with a squadron of Zeros (Japanese fighter planes) poised to protect the remote island and its treasure. When the air battle ended, the American planes had done their duty and the Japanese were never able to retrieve a single shipment of phosphate ore from Nauru. But *Super Man* limped back to its air base on the equatorial island of Canton with 594 bullet holes riddling the plane from front to back. The crew of *Super Man* didn't really believe they would make it. The plane was shot to pieces and the hydraulics were nonexistent, which meant the landing gear was inoperative. The maneuverability of the aircraft was questionable because the flaps were shot up, and the last piece of the equation for a successful return to base was fuel. When the aircraft finally did land, it was running "on fumes."

However, Harry Brooks and three other crewmen had been hit by Zero fire during the air battle, and all were seriously injured. On the limping flight back to base, Harry Brooks lay unconscious. He had two holes in the back of his skull. Even though Harry Brooks made it to the hospital barracks once the plane made an emergency landing, he did not make it through surgery. Tech Sergeant Harold Brooks died that day, one week before his twenty-third birthday. It took more than a week for word to reach Harry's mother at 511 ½ Western Avenue in Clarksville, Michigan. On the other side of Clarksville, Jeannette Burtscher, Harry's fiancé, also learned of his death—just nine days before the wedding date she and Harry had set before he left for war.[20] Harry Brooks sacrificed his life. Harry's mother sacrificed a son. Harry's fiancé sacrificed a future husband and the love of her life.

Often we think about sacrifice in war as related to direct combat situations. It is important to realize that, in World War II, as well as all wars and even peacetime, men and women throughout the history of the United States made sacrifices simply because they were located in dangerous areas or were involved in programs designed to help a particular war effort, but their sacrifices were not a direct result of combat.

One example, which is related to Louie Zamperini's story, is the crewmen who flew the B-24 Liberator bombers. The training was almost as dangerous as combat. When newly designed aircraft are tested, especially during a war, the process is often accelerated to get the tested aircraft into the war as soon as possible. In the case of the B-24 during World War II, 35,933 aircraft were in combat and test accidents. The surprising statistic is that only a fraction of the aircraft were lost in combat. In the Pacific campaign in 1943 only, for every plane lost in combat, six were lost in accidents related to mechanical malfunction, pilot error, and even accidents involving other aircraft (friendly fire). Combat losses of life never outnumbered non-combat losses of life. Over the course of the war in the army air corps, 35,946 personnel died in non-combat situations. In a report issued by the AAF surgeon general, between November 1, 1943 and May 25, 1945, 70 percent of the men listed as killed in action died in operational aircraft accidents, not as a result of enemy action.[21]

Consider this: on February 28, 1942, the USS *Houston* engaged the Japanese navy in what came to be known as the Battle of Sunda Strait in the Java Sea area of the south Pacific. The Australian vessel, the HMAS *Perth,* also engaged the Japanese navy alongside the *Houston*. Both vessels were sunk. The *Houston* lost 693 men and the *Perth* lost 353 sailors. Many who survived went to Japanese prison camps.[22]

At 12:14 a.m. on July 30, 1945, the USS *Indianapolis* was torpedoed by a Japanese submarine in the Philippine Sea. The ship sunk in twelve minutes. The *Indianapolis* was returning from an ultra-secret mission that had delivered the atomic bomb to the island of Tinian. One week later, the *Enola Gay* would drop that bomb on Hiroshima, Japan. Of the 1,196 men on board the *Indianapolis*, approximately 300 went down with the ship. The remaining 900 men were left floating for days in the shark-infested waters of the south Pacific. The mission had been so secretive that the navy did not even list the ship as missing for three days. By the time the survivors in the waters were spotted four days later, only 316 survived. The rest had died of exposure or had been eaten by tiger sharks.[23]

These were only three ships out of hundreds that were involved in combat during World War II. Many other ships were sunk or damaged in battle. Thousands of other navy men lost their lives in combat. Sacrifice. Remember, there is an individual story for every serviceman and servicewoman who lost his or her life. Each one had dreams. Every one had family and friends back home. Every one had a life to live. Each life lost was a life cut short. Every life lost was a life sacrificed. But every death had a purpose. There was a greater cause and a greater purpose. There are thousands of stories of personal sacrifice.

So what does this mean? That the sacrifice of the men who died in non-combat situations was less meaningful than the sacrifice made by men in combat? Of course not! The men who died in non-combat situations were risking their lives daily just by operating and testing the aircraft that would eventually be flown in combat areas. It could actually be argued that the men flying the test aircraft were responsible for saving a vast number of lives of men who would eventually fly in combat because of the knowledge gained from their test experience and data gathered from the tests, which often resulted in death.

As I write about these courageous exploits, I almost feel guilty because I mentioned so few examples of courage and selfless dedication. To write about all those who daily put their lives on the line would take volumes, and my purpose is to focus on the concept of sacrifice. These stories of gallantry and sacrifice in the turbulent years of World War II are almost endless. To put it in some perspective, consider the following facts:

- Not every soldier who sacrificed earned a medal.
- America's highest military award is the Congressional Medal of Honor.
- In World War II there were 440 Medal of Honor recipients.

- Two hundred fifty of the recipients were awarded the Medal of Honor posthumously.
- Every recipient of the Medal of Honor had a story of valor and sacrifice.
- The Congressional Medal of Honor has been awarded to 3,457 Americans. Today, only 85 of them survive.

Private Robert D. Booker was one such Congressional Medal of Honor recipient. Private Booker, an infantryman with the Thirty-Fourth Army Infantry Division was stationed in North Africa in 1944. On April 9, 1943, in the vicinity of Fondouk, Tunisia, Private Booker displayed heroic and sacrificial action while engaging enemy forces. He was wounded while carrying a machine gun and ammunition more than two hundred yards while advancing on two enemy machine gun nests and mortar emplacements. Private Booker silenced one enemy machine gun and had begun firing on the other when he was mortally wounded. Even in his seriously wounded state, Robert Booker continued to encourage his squad, directing their fire on the enemy.[24]

Private Robert Booker is only one of the 440 stories of the Congressional Medal of Honor recipients during World War II. The death toll, military and civilian, for World War II was approximately 70 million. The most expansive and costly war in human history contains millions of untold stories of sacrifice.

My father-in-law is one of the untold stories. Charles Duane Setser entered the army in March 1943. He was eighteen. His twin brother, Chase, entered the service also in March 1943. Chase was a marine who served in the Pacific theater. On the island of Tarawa, Chase was a member of an eight-man communication team. Four of the eight men were killed. The three-day battle in November 1943 cost America the lives of more than one thousand marines. Chase Setser was one of the lucky survivors of Tarawa.

Charles's older brother, Paul Setser, had entered the Marine Corps in September 1942. Although Paul served in different locations in the Pacific, his most hostile and dangerous action came in the Battle of Okinawa, which I referenced earlier in this chapter. On one occasion, Paul was under intense enemy fire and jumped into a foxhole and landed on top of another marine. Much to his surprise, the marine on whom he landed was a friend from Columbus, Indiana. Neither man had any idea the other was in the same theater of war. Paul was lucky also. The Battle of Okinawa lasted three months, and America lost more than twelve thousand marines in that battle. More than forty thousand were wounded. Paul came home alive without serious injury.

But back to my father-in-law. Charles Setser did not serve in the Pacific war. He was shipped to the European theater. Shipping out of Newport News, Virginia, in late November 1943, Charles was among thousands who were heading to North Africa. In cramped quarters and often seasick, they headed for a twenty-three-day voyage that took them to the port of Oran, Algeria, in North Africa. The convoy was made up of what was called "Liberty Ships" for transporting troops. According to Charles, the ships zigzagged every seven minutes to avoid German submarines. Evidently, it took eight minutes to set up to fire torpedoes, so changing course every seven minutes was absolutely necessary. This submarine prevention maneuvering lengthened the duration of the voyage by several days.

Eventually, after a month of training in Algeria, his group was attached to the Forty-Fifth Infantry Division of the Fifth US Army command under General Mark Clark near Naples, Italy. Charles was sent to the front lines trying to hold the line at Cassina, where combat raged for several months. In the middle of this battle, Winston Churchill, consulting with the Americans, decided to pull the Forty-Fifth Division and send them to the Anzio beachhead.

According to notes written by Charles, he said, "But on February 17, 1944, about one thousand to fifteen hundred of our troops were captured. I'll never forget my platoon leader and I were captured by a big Mark VI German tank commanded by the only redheaded German soldier I ever saw." It sounded funny at the time when Charles told me the story. He laughed a little telling me about it. But get serious—at the time it was no laughing matter. Charles and his platoon leader were staring death in the face at the end of the machine gun on that German Mark VI tank. Charles and other American combat prisoners were taken to Rome, Italy, where they spent twenty-one days in a POW camp.

On March 10, 1944, they were herded like cattle on German prison trucks and transported to another prison camp in Laterina, Italy. Soldiers from many nations occupied this camp: Australians, Russians, British, as well as Americans. This camp was well staffed with many guards and German shepherd attack dogs. Barbed wire encircled the camp. Charles recalled sleeping on lice-infested straw. He was in this camp for about four months, never changing clothes. He would only pull his pants down for two reasons—to go the latrine (primitive, as you might guess) and to kill the "big, gray-back lice." It was here, in the Laterina camp, that Charles's leg became infected from the lice bites. Over time his leg got worse and he was finally given minimal medical attention as a POW in Germany. To this day, Charles walks with a limp and wears a brace to support his "bad leg."

Rations were sparse also—one loaf of black bread each day for six men. Constipation was obviously a problem. At the end of the four months, the American soldiers were loaded on a train into cattle box cars (about forty feet by eight feet). The troops were crowded so tightly that they had to alternate standing and sitting to rest. The Americans were in the cattle cars for three days and two nights. Barbed wire was strung across openings, allowing for ventilation. There were no lights. The restroom was a wooden box with sawdust in it. At one point after exiting the Brenner Pass in the Alps between Italy and Austria, the train had to be stopped because of air attacks by Allied planes. They stopped the train and backed into the mountain tunnel. The train was on the way to Stalag 7A in Moosburg, Germany. Moosburg was the largest German POW camp housing, at its peak, well more than one hundred thousand Allied POWs.

When the camp was liberated in 1945, it was estimated that more than 110,000 Allied POWs were there. From Moosburg, POWs were sent out on daily work details usually digging ditches, obviously under armed guard.

However, Charles and some others were later transported to Memmingen, Germany (Bavaria). From there, eighteen POWs, who had grown up on American farms, were sent to a nearby farm community to do farm work. There were POW barracks located at Memmingen, which had held French prisoners during World War I. Charles said there were still bars on the windows. Rations were skimpy—a Red Cross parcel once a month consisting of about ten pounds of food was basically all they had to eat. Charles said they would have starved to death if it were not for the Red Cross food packages.

In March 1945, Charles and the other POWs were evacuated to another camp because the American troops were rapidly closing in. Shortly thereafter, in early May 1945, the guards of the POW camp threw open the gates, saluted the POWs, and left in a hurry.

Setser brothers, WWII veterans: Back row, second from right: Charles, Anzio; third from right Chase, Tarawa; and third from left Paul, Okinawa. Photo taken in 2007.

What are the odds that three brothers, all fighting in heavy combat situations where casualties were heavy, all came back alive and without serious injury? Considering the battles at Tarawa, Okinawa, and Anzio, I think the odds are quite small. I'm sure the Setser brothers, as well as multiple thousands of other US troops who were caught up in the world at war of the 1940s, would not consider themselves heroes. There were hundreds of thousands, perhaps millions of Americans who fought in the Pacific and European theaters of World War II. If you were to ask those veterans today about who the real heroes were, the typical answer is, "The real heroes are the ones who did not come back." But all of them sacrificed because all of them did their duty and served their country, all for human freedom during what could arguably be called the darkest era in world history.

There are untold stories of sacrifice by men and women who were not recipients of medals. There are stories that were never recorded and stories that are known only to God. Yet even in the lowest ebb of human degradation and cruelty that war can provide, there are stories of what is considered the best of the human spirit, such as stories of selfless sacrifice, even unto death, for the good of others. For the good of their "brothers in arms." For the good of their country. For the good of their families and loved ones. For the good of oppressed people. How can we forget them? We cannot! We must remember their names, their endeavors, their selfless actions, their sacrifice!

Every single day approximately one thousand World War II veterans die. Most are now in their eighties and nineties. If you have a living relative or you know someone who served in World War II, take the time to thank him for his service and sacrifice. Then ask yourself a simple question: "What can I do to sacrifice for my country?"

Chapter 2

Another Time, Another Place

Heroes and sacrifice are not limited to World War II. The calamitous years of the Second World War were certainly fertile ground for heroic and sacrificial acts. After all, the world was under the shadow of evil despots with visions of complete world power and domination. But the history of the United States is fraught with sacrificial acts that are just as brave and just as sacrificial as those that occurred during World War II. But my purpose is not to recount every sacrificial and heroic act throughout the history of our great country. That would be an impossible task. But I will continue to give some examples relevant to the subject of sacrifice.

The American Revolution is well-documented and has its lengthy cast of heroes. Who has not heard of, read about, and marveled at the courageous and sacrificial acts of George Washington, Nathaniel Green, Samuel Adams, John Adams, Thomas Jefferson, Francis Marian, and a host of other Revolutionary War characters who were heroes who made monumental sacrifices that benefited many in the American colonies? But have you ever heard of Haym Salomon? This man made sacrificial acts of life and fortune. And although his personal actions were not on the battlefield, they were certainly just as important for the American cause of freedom and liberty.

In the midst of our American culture today, living in the most blessed nation on the face of the earth, living in a secure society where laws enacted by the people rule over our land and where we have the freedom to choose our own path in life, do we ever consider that in the winter of 1776 George Washington and his band of colonial firebrands were hanging on by their fingernails? Do we ever consider that they were facing an almost certain death at the hands of the British? Do we ever really think of the hardship and sacrifice faced by those who took up the cause of freedom in the year the Declaration of Independence was drafted?

On Christmas Day 1776, many colonial leaders were worried that the war being fought for the independence of the American colonies was all but lost. But there were those, few in number as they were, who still believed in the cause of freedom and were determined to follow through, no matter what the cost, to win that freedom. George Washington, commander of the continental army, was the dominant military leader of the colonies and would later become the most dominant political leader of the upstart democracy. On that awful Christmas night, now more than 230 years ago, Washington led his army through a winter storm of rain, sleet, ice, and snow to a victory over the British at Trenton. Easy, right? Did you ever try to cross a wide river in the middle of winter at midnight in freezing temperatures without light of any kind? The crossing alone was extremely treacherous. But then, Washington's band of ragtag colonials, many literally dressed in rags, or as noted American historian David McCullough phrased it, "the men were in tatters, many without shoes, their feet wrapped in rags."[1] These disheveled colonials marched nine miles over frozen ground to win a surprise attack victory over the British. Thomas Paine wrote, "These are the times that try men's souls." That was an understatement. Washington's crossing of the Delaware that Christmas night is truly a cornerstone event in the history of our nation. His little army of maybe two thousand men, in absolutely terrible winter conditions, pulled off the impossible. The colonial army captured more than one thousand Hessian mercenaries and moved on to win a decisive battle against British regular troops at Princeton shortly thereafter.

But Washington's army was to face an even harsher environment the following winter. We've all heard about Valley Forge. Washington's troops wintered at Valley Forge, keeping an eye on the British army, which occupied Philadelphia. The winter was brutal to say the least. Over the next few months, the colonial troops at Valley Forge, originally numbering more than eleven thousand, dwindled to about two-thirds that number due to disease and exposure. His army, despite lack of food, proper shelter, and medical supplies endured that winter and fought the British in a major battle at Monmouth, New Jersey, on June 28, 1778. Washington and his colonials continued to follow and badger the British all the way to New York. With financial and military help from the French, Washington was able to bring the Revolutionary War to a close when his army, along with help from the French navy blockading the Virginia coastline, surrounded the British under General Cornwallis at Yorktown, Virginia, in October 1781.

Sacrifice for a cause? Suffering, near-starvation, extreme cold, no medical supplies, staring death in the face on a daily basis. Washington and his colonial troops sacrificed beyond our wildest imagination. And today we reap the fruits of their sacrifice. Washington and his dedicated troops certainly changed the course of world history. They willfully forged a free nation, and we have inherited the blessings of their sacrifices.

Haym Salomon was a Polish Jew who never fought in a military campaign. He played a major role in the financing segment of the American Revolution. He was actually arrested by the British as a spy in 1776 but was acquitted, only to be arrested again in 1778 and sentenced to death. As you can surmise, his actions and the resulting sentence of death were no small matters. Salomon escaped and arrived in Philadelphia as the Continental Congress was struggling to raise money to support the war. Congress had no powers of direct taxation and had to rely on requests for money directed to the states, which were mostly refused. The government had no choice but to borrow money and was ultimately bailed out only by loans from the French and Dutch governments. Government finances were in a chaotic state in 1781 when Congress appointed former Congressman Robert Morris superintendent of finance. The Bank of North America was created and proceeded to finance the Yorktown campaign of Washington and the French General Jean-Baptiste Rochambeau. The new superintendent of finance relied on public-spirited financiers like Salomon to subscribe to the bank, find purchasers for government bills of exchange, and lend personal money to the fledgling government. From 1781 on, Salomon brokered bills of exchange for the American government and extended interest-free personal loans to members of Congress, including James Madison. So within five years of his arrival in Philadelphia, Salomon moved from an impoverished fugitive to a respected businessman and financier. Haym Salomon risked his life and his fortune pledging himself to the Revolutionary cause. He died bankrupt in 1785 having made selfless contributions to the ideals and the success of the American Revolution.[2]

Likewise, in a pre-US territory historical venue, the movement for Texas independence produced a heroic and sacrificial stand at the Alamo Mission near San Antonio de Béxar (modern-day San Antonio, Texas). On March 6, 1836, in a defensive stand at the old Spanish mission, the Texans took a suicidal stand against the Mexican army under President General Antonio López de Santa Anna. The Mexican army numbered close to 2,500 against a small force estimated between 182 and 257 Texans led by Colonel William Travis and frontiersman Jim Bowie. The legendary Davy Crockett and a few volunteers he had gathered also joined the Texans before the final engagement with the Mexican army. The Texans were buying time for Sam Houston to organize an army and secure supplies to fight the Mexican army in the battle for an independent Texas. Meanwhile, an independent Texas government and new constitution were being organized, but not at any small cost. Lives were sacrificed for a cause—the cause of freedom for future generations. We all know the story and the outcome. Sam Houston formed the army, and on April 21, 1836, Houston and his Texan army, with the battle cry "Remember the Alamo," defeated Santa Anna's Mexican army at the Battle of San Jacinto. The Texas government was established, and Texas eventually became an independent republic later to be annexed as the twenty-eighth state of the Union in 1845.

Hundreds of thousands—actually, one estimate is 625,000—Americans lost their lives in the Civil War. That averages to about 600 deaths per day. Sacrifice in this American tragedy was an everyday occurrence. To select representative stories of sacrifice would be a difficult task because there were just so many. However, one story is unique. It is the story of a fourteen-year-old drummer boy named William Horsfall. He was a Kentucky youngster who felt the urge of patriotism when the Civil War began. He stowed away on a riverboat and finally made it into a federal regiment. He must have lied about his age. Ultimately, fighting near Corinth, Mississippi, young Horsfall, now fifteen, disregarded his own safety to save his regimental captain's life. Young Horsfall wrote, "The regiment had just made a desperate charge across the ravine. Captain Williamson was wounded in the charge and, in subsequent reversing of positions, was left between the lines ... so I ... in a stooping run, gained his side and dragged him to the stretcher bearers, who took him to the rear."[3] This act of courage won William Horsfall the Congressional Medal of Honor, making him the nation's youngest recipient of that prestigious honor.

To even consider the sacrifices made in the American Civil War is a staggering thought. All kinds of statistics are available, but an estimate based on factual data suggests the total deaths suffered by the Union army were 360,222 and the Confederate army's total deaths were 258,000.[4]

How many acts of valor and sacrifice can be counted in this hellish war? And what about Abraham Lincoln himself? He is counted as the most revered of all US presidents in nearly every poll. Did he sacrifice his life? Did he take seriously the death and destruction that was a plague on the United States of America from 1861 to 1865? Of course he did! Look at his photographs during the war years. He aged twenty years in a period of four years. And do you think there was not a day that passed that he didn't think he might be the target of an assassin's bullet? And eventually that day came. He knew the dangers. He is the only US president who served nearly his entire term in the White House with enemy forces less than one hundred miles from his home and enemy spies lingering near his every move.

However, there is one Civil War combatant who deserves mention because of her sacrifice. Yes, I said "her." Clara Barton's Civil War work began immediately after the First Battle of Bull Run in 1861. She formed a group for the purpose of obtaining and then distributing medical supplies to the war's wounded. She did not stop there. A year later she obtained permission to give direct aid to wounded soldiers, Union and Confederate alike, behind battle lines. Eventually, she and her cadre of nurses traveled to some of the bloodiest battlefields of the war, including the battles for Petersburg and Richmond, Virginia. Of course we know that she founded the American Red Cross, which still comes to the aid of millions in distress every year. Dr. James Dunn, a surgeon at the horrific battle of Antietam, said of Clara Barton, "In my feeble estimation, General McClellan, with all his laurels, sinks into insignificance beside the true heroine of the age, the angel of the battlefield."[5] (If you are not aware, the battle of Antietam was the bloodiest single-day battle of the Civil War. The battle has been described as "wholesale butchery." Though gory beyond description and terrible in its human cost [approximately thirty-eight thousand casualties in a single day], the result of the battle has been defined as a "defeat for both armies.")[6]

Clara Barton witnessed human suffering in a period where war produced the worst kinds of injury and mutilation with medical techniques, equipment, supplies, and untrained personnel that were far behind the advancements in military weaponry. In short, most of us cannot imagine the horrors Clara Barton witnessed and the helplessness she must have felt in situations that would make most of us get sick to our stomachs and walk away muttering, "I can't take this!" Clara Barton dedicated her life to the service of those who were wounded, dying and living in terrible conditions. She served as the director of the American Red Cross until her death in 1912.

"In addition to performing gallantly the duties pertaining to his position, voluntarily and unaided carried several seriously wounded men from the firing line to a secure position in the rear, in each instance being subjected to a very heavy fire and great exposure and danger."[7] These are the words on his Medal of Honor citation. James Robb Church was not your typical soldier who won a Congressional Medal of Honor. Actually, he was not a soldier at all. James Robb was an assistant army surgeon stationed in Cuba in the Spanish-American War. He also served as an attaché to the French army in World War I. He was an author and a doctor. He is buried in Arlington National Cemetery. A doctor, risking his life under enemy fire to rescue wounded soldiers during battle? The doctor was as much a soldier as he was a surgeon. The lesson for us here is that our calling in life is not what is most important; when duty demands that we take risks, great or small, even life-threatening risks, our occupation does not matter. People matter.

The year was 1918, less than a year before the world's worst military cataclysm to that point in time, would come to a merciful end. A Tennessee blacksmith and farmer by the name of Alvin York became an American hero in the First World War. Sergeant Alvin C. York, a native of the Tennessee Mountains, a renown rifle sharpshooter and pistol marksman became known as the extraordinary hero of the Argonne Battle. "There is no story of the great war that reads more like an extravagant fiction; but thoroughly attested, its truth unquestionably established by official investigation and by the sworn statements of fellow soldiers as one of the most amazing individual achievements in the four years crowded with deeds of almost incredible heroism and daring."[8]

Sergeant York, a member of Company G of the 328 Infantry, 28th Division of the American Expeditionary Force, during operations in the Argonne Forest district of France, accomplished what has become known as one of the most amazing feats in military history. Alvin York, acting completely alone, captured 132 prisoners, including a major and several lieutenants, and put out of commission thirty-five machine guns subduing the machine gun battalion with his rifle and automatic pistol. For his monumental act of bravery the French government in the person of Marshal Foch awarded York the French Croix de Guerre (Cross of War), a French military decoration for heroism. Upon arrival back in the states, York was awarded the Congressional Medal of Honor.

Army nurse Helen Fairchild was in the military hospital near the battle front for the Third Battle of Ypres-Passchendaele, which was fought from July through November 1917 in Belgium. To give some perspective, this World War I battle was so expansive that more than five hundred thousand casualties were incurred by both sides in this battle alone. "Fairchild was one of sixty-four nurses from Pennsylvania Hospital Unit #10 who had volunteered to join the American Expeditionary Force after the United States entered World War I on April 6, 1917. She was not destined to tell the stories she mentioned. Nurse Fairchild died on Jan. 8, 1918, while on duty with British Base Hospital #10/#16."[9] She was one of sixty-four nurses who were responsible for the care of more than two thousand beds crammed with war wounded needing immediate and critical attention as well as assisting in the daily surgeries that were necessary.

The only glamour in war comes from movies and TV. Any war veteran, especially those who have served in life-threatening combat, will tell you that war is horrible and unforgettable. I'm certain the sights seen by Nurse Fairchild (and all other military nurses in war zones) would make most of us squeamish and probably faint. Chief Nurse Julia Stimson wrote of all the nurses endured: "What with the steam, the ether … the odor in the operating room … sewing and tying up and putting in drains while the doctor takes the next piece of shell out … Then after fourteen hours of this … off to rest if you can … one need never tell me that women can't do as much, stand as much, and be as brave as men."[10] Nell Fairchild Rote, the niece of Helen Fairchild, said she received a letter from a nurse who was then a captain in the US Air Force: "Helen's story reached across the years and spoke to the very moment in which I was training," wrote Lynn Nicklas Stepaniak. "Her story portrays the purest form of sacrifice." The young nurse Helen Fairchild, who would have "books to tell" when she returned home, still inspires by her example.[11]

The key word in Lynn Stepaniak's tribute to Helen Fairchild is "sacrifice." Nurse Fairchild's unwavering commitment, loyalty, service, and especially her love and caring for those brave young men who were caught in the ravenous jaws of World War I is the true meaning of personal sacrifice.

Why do people, average, everyday working people, people who are not soldiers by training or vocation, why do these people sacrifice everything or at least take risky actions that could result in sacrificing one's life? Example? We've already mentioned several. But what about Nathan Hale? Oh sure, he was a hero during the Revolutionary War, right? He must have been a soldier fighting for the colonial cause, right? Not really! Remember his words spoken just before his execution on September 22, 1776? "I only regret that I have but one life to lose for my country!" Yes, Nathan Hale, along with his five brothers, joined the revolutionary cause in 1776, but they were certainly not trained soldiers. Nathan Hale was a school teacher. His brothers fought at the early battles of Lexington and Concord on April 19, 1775. He joined them on July 1 of the same year. Nathan soon became a captain and fought with George Washington in that nasty New York campaign against British General William Howe. General Washington asked for volunteers to go on a spy mission to find and assess the position and strength of Howe's troops. Nathan Hale volunteered. Nathan Hale was captured returning to the colonial troops from his spy mission. The British found papers on his person confirming he was spying on the British.[12]

We've all studied the American Revolution to a greater or lesser degree. And we know that many acts leading to and having a lasting impact upon that revolution occurred long before 1776. Actually, there was not one signer of the Declaration of Independence who did not take great risk or experience great personal sacrifice before, during, or after the American Revolution. Remember, the very act of signing the Declaration of Independence made them traitors, disloyal to King George and to England. At that time in history, treason under English law, as it is in our own country today, carried the penalty of death.

It has been truly stated, "There is nothing greater than the heart of a volunteer." A volunteer steps forward because of a belief in a cause. Nathan Hale was a volunteer. Actually George Washington, all the signers of the Declaration of Independence, practically all who sacrificed for the American Colonies were volunteers to a greater or lesser degree. The very definition of the word volunteer is "to offer or give of one's free will," which inherently implies sacrifice at some level.[13] As American citizens, true patriots at heart, we must ask ourselves, "In what ways or by what means can I volunteer to serve my country? How can I sacrifice for my country and for my fellow countrymen?" Can the commitment and patriotism that existed in the hearts of the signers of the Declaration of Independence still live in the hearts of Americans today? If we read the words of the founding document of the United States, signed on July 4, 1776, I think we can rekindle the commitment to sacrifice found in those words of idealism and hope. Read the Declaration of Independence every once in a while. You will be inspired and amazed at the God-inspired words penned there, providing the foundation of freedom in human government.

Chapter 3

Unpopular Sacrifices

No war should be popular. But if war is necessary, it should have a clear purpose related to national security. The most unpopular war in the history of the United States was undoubtedly the Vietnam War. American military advisers to the French actually started arriving in South Vietnam about 1950, only five years after the fall of Nazi Germany. The major concern for the United States was the fear of Communist aggression in Southeast Asia. North Vietnam was communist and South Vietnam, although considered a free nation, was thought to be a puppet state of the French in its last days of international imperialism. Regardless of the politics, boundary lines were being drawn for what was to become a costly war for the United States in terms of money and human lives.

The Vietnam War accounted for approximately fifty-eight thousand American military deaths from 1965-74. Comparatively, the United States lost more than one hundred thousand men in World War I (1917-1918), more than four hundred thousand in World War II (1941-45), and more than thirty-five thousand in the Korean War (1950-53). But the Vietnam War was unique in its own right, and lasting nearly a decade with nightly TV news reporting killed, missing, and wounded numbers on a daily basis, America soon became tired of the heavy losses for what was a questionable cause so far from the home shores of America.

But don't let the unpopularity of the Vietnam War diminish in any way the actions and sacrifices of those who served bravely and with dedication in that faraway land of southeast Asia. Americans who served in Vietnam must still be remembered with respect and an attitude of thankfulness for their efforts to stop the aggression posed by the communist dictatorships that were trying to take southeast Asia hostage in that era. There were many Americans in the Vietnam conflict who sacrificed immeasurably and should be remembered for their gallantry, service, and sacrifice.

On October 26, 1967, he was flying his twenty-third bombing mission over North Vietnam when his A-4E Skyhawk, flying off the carrier USS *Oriskany,* under OPERATION ROLLING THUNDER (the bombing campaign over North Vietnam) was shot down by a North Vietnamese missile over Hanoi. Lieutenant Commander John McCain was seriously injured ejecting from the aircraft. He fractured both arms and a leg and nearly drowned when he parachuted into a lake. Some North Vietnamese citizens pulled him out of the water, where he was assaulted by an angry mob ... "shouting wildly at me, stripping my clothes off, spitting on me, kicking and striking me repeatedly. Someone smashed a rifle butt into my right shoulder, breaking it. Someone else stuck a bayonet in my right ankle and groin."[1] McCain was then transported to Hanoi's main Hoa Lo Prison, better known as the "Hanoi Hilton."

Although McCain was badly wounded, his North Vietnamese captors refused to medically treat him. He was beaten and interrogated routinely and ruthlessly to get information. He was given medical care only when the North Vietnamese discovered his father was an admiral in the US Navy. He became a bargaining chip, and his status as a POW was front page news in all the major newspapers. Now with the communist media involved, McCain spent six weeks in the hospital while receiving marginal care. By then, having lost fifty pounds while restricted in a chest cast, and with his hair turned white, he was sent to a different camp on the outskirts of Hanoi in December 1967. He was placed in a cell with two other Americans, who did not expect him to live a week. In March 1968 McCain was put into solitary confinement, where he would remain for two years. "At nine o'clock every evening, the guards rang the evening gong instructing us to go to sleep, and shivering in the cold or sweating in the stifling heat, beset by mosquitoes, and in the glare of a naked lightbulb, we tried to escape into our dreams."[2]

After a botched escape attempt from the prison in 1969, things got even worse. In retribution for an attempted escape, in John McCain's own words: "Our treatment reached its nadir … reprisals were ordered at every [POW] camp. Many prisoners were tortured to reveal other escape plans. Beatings were inflicted for even minor infractions of prison rules. The food was worse. Security was tightened and our cells were frequently and thoroughly inspected. Many of us suffered from boils—in the sweltering heat, our lymph glands clogged up and baseball-sized boils developed under our arms. All we had to treat them with was small vials of iodine."

Attempting to communicate with other prisoners was strictly forbidden. Lt. Commander McCain, as well as many others, were caught in such attempts. McCain said he was beaten several times for such efforts. On another occasion, McCain was made to stand facing a wall for two days and two nights. Exhausted, on the second day he sat down. Mistaken for insolence, the guard beat him mercilessly and jumped on his wounded leg.[3]

John McCain's POW imprisonment continued until March 1973. President Nixon escalated the B-52 bombing raids on North Vietnam in 1972, which certainly sped up the release of POWs. On March 15, 1973, Lieutenant Commander McCain and several other POWs were released and began the journey home. His wartime injuries prevented him then, and for the rest of his life, from raising his arms above his head.

The history of the Vietnam War is full of heroic acts and sacrificial deeds. Lieutenant Colonel Harold (Hal) Moore served in Japan following World War II, in the Korean War, and was best known for his gallantry in the earliest campaign of the Vietnam War. In 1954, while serving as an instructor at West Point, Moore taught cadet Norman Schwarzkopf, who called Moore one of his "heroes," and cites Moore as the reason he chose the infantry branch upon graduation. Schwarzkopf later became a general and led the UN Coalition forces in the 1991 Gulf War. In 1964, Lieutenant Colonel Moore completed the course of study at the National War College, while earning a master's degree in International Affairs from George Washington University. Moore was transferred to Fort Benning, Georgia, and commanded a battalion in the Eleventh Air Assault Division, undergoing air assault and air mobility training and tests until July 1965, when the division was renamed the First Cavalry Division.

It was at this point that Hal Moore took his unit to South Vietnam to "try out" the new technique of dropping ground troops into "enemy hot zones" with helicopters. The helicopters would shuttle in troops and supplies to support the ground effort and tactics. This was the case in November 1965, at the Battle of Ia Drang Valley. The United

States lost 240 infantry, with 470 wounded and 6 missing in action; November 17 was the deadliest ambush for Americans in the entire Vietnam War, with 155 men killed and 126 men wounded. The battle highlighted a record number of North Vietnamese casualties—2,262 dead, nearly 2,000 wounded, and 136 captured. The encounter was one of the first times in the war that the North Vietnamese (Viet Cong) kept attacking American units despite heavy losses, instead of stealing away.

Lieutenant Colonel Moore took his unit: the First Battalion, Seventh US Cavalry (then in the Third Brigade Combat Team, First Cavalry Division) to South Vietnam, and led it in the famous Battle of Ia Drang. Encircled by enemy soldiers, with no clear landing zone (LZ) that would allow them to leave, Moore managed to persevere despite overwhelming odds. A sister battalion only two-and-a-half miles away was massacred the next day. Moore's dictum that "there is always one more thing you can do to increase your odds of success," and the courage of his entire command are credited with this astounding outcome. Moore's spirited defense led to more than a four-to-one ratio between North Vietnamese casualties and US casualties in their first major engagement of the war. In his career, Lieutenant General Hal Moore earned more than thirty active duty service medals honoring his actions.[4]

On April 10, 2010, at the Army Aviation Convention held in Fort Worth, Texas, President George W. Bush presented the Congressional Medal of Honor, the nation's highest honor for military service, to Lieutenant Colonel Bruce Crandall. In 1965, then Major Crandall led sixteen helicopter crews of the First Cavalry Division that extracted troops from search and destroy missions from Plei Me to Landing Zone X-Ray in what would become known as the most heated fight in the Vietnam War to date—the Battle of Ia Drang Valley, November 14-16, 1965.

It was Lieutenant Colonel Hal Moore's ground troops that depended on Crandall's helicopters to insert soldiers into the battle. It was during the fifth troop lift under torrential enemy fire that Crandall's helicopter landed and ground forces left the copter. Three soldiers were immediately wounded and three were killed. All the remaining helicopters waiting to land with additional troops were ordered to abort their landings. Major Crandall returned to base to find that medical evacuation landings had been stopped due to the ferocity and danger of the battle in the landing area. Major Crandall made the immediate decision to fly medical evacuation missions back to the battle area. Volunteering to join him was Major Ed Freeman, a friend for ten years. Colonel John Herren said of Crandall (and Freeman), "They evacuated our wounded and brought in water and ammunition, despite intense enemy fire. These helicopters were our lifeline. It demonstrated to me and other soldiers in the field that our casualties were going to be taken care of and that they would not have to wait for a break in the fighting to be evacuated."[5]

Additionally, one of Herron's platoons was cut off for twenty-four hours and suffered twenty casualties. Every one of the wounded survived because Crandall and Freeman evacuated them. Of thirty-one helicopter loads of ammunition and supplies brought into the LZ (landing zone) after it was closed, Crandall and Freeman's helicopter brought in twenty-eight. And of the approximately seventy-eight wounded in action who were evacuated, Crandall's helicopter took out seventy.

Jack Smith was also there those terrible three days in November 1965. Jack Smith is, for those of you younger than fifty, the son of former ABC national news correspondent Howard K. Smith (ABC News 1962-79). Jack Smith wrote and spoke extensively about the Battle of Ia Drang Valley. He passed away on April 7, 2004, more than likely from overexposure to the defoliant Agent Orange, which was used prolifically in Vietnam to kill jungle vegetation where the Vietcong were hiding. In a speech given on November 8, 2003, at a banquet in Crystal City, Virginia, honoring the survivors of the Battle of Ia Drang Valley, Jack Smith said, "I have pancreatic cancer. If it is Agent Orange, it's not the first time this ... war has tried to kill me."[6]

Being the son of a former war correspondent and a veteran national news commentator, Jack was a stickler for detail. Remembering like it was yesterday, Jack told his audience of the awful statistics that were a result of the battle. The fighting was hand-to-hand. He said he was lying so close to a North Vietnamese machine gunner that he simply stuck out his rifle and blew off his head. Smith reported it was the only time during the war that a US battalion was ever overrun. He reported, "The First Battalion had been fighting continuously for three or four days, and I had never seen such filthy troops. Some of them had blood on their faces from scratches and from other guys' wounds. Some had long rips in their clothing where shrapnel and bullets had missed them. They all had that look of shock. They said little, just looked around with darting, nervous eyes. I heard the casualty figures a few days later. The North Vietnamese unit had been wiped out—more than 500 dead. Out of some 500 men in our battalion alone, about 150 had been killed, and only 84 returned to base camp a few days later. In my company, which was right in the middle of the ambush, we had 93 percent casualties—one half dead, one half wounded. Almost all the wounded were crippled for life. The company, in fact, was very nearly annihilated. Our unit is part of the Seventh Cavalry, George Armstrong Custer's old unit. That day in the Ia Drang Valley, history repeated itself."[7]

Like John McCain, Captain Lance P. Sijan was a resident of the "Hanoi Hilton." The difference was that having been shot down in a similar manner as Lieutenant Colonel McCain, Sijan avoided capture for several weeks. Once captured and placed in a small POW camp, Captain Sijan was able to overpower a guard and escape. He was recaptured within hours, and after several days was eventually transferred to Hanoi. After only ten days in another POW camp, Sijan and two other pilots were transferred to the infamous "Hanoi Hilton." His injuries neglected, and starved and tortured, Sijan refused to accede to his captors' demands for information. On January 22, 1968, Lance Sijan died.[8] In his Medal of Honor citation, it says regarding Captain Sijan's final days, "During interrogation, he was severely tortured; however, he did not divulge any information to his captors. Capt. Sijan lapsed into delirium and was placed in the care of another prisoner. During his intermittent periods of consciousness until his death, he never complained of his physical condition and on several occasions spoke of future escape attempts. Capt. Sijan's extraordinary heroism and intrepidity above and beyond the call of duty at the cost of his life are in keeping with the highest traditions of the US Air Force and reflect great credit upon himself and the US Armed Forces."[9]

On April 1, 1970, another story of heroism and sacrifice became history. Sergeant Peter Lemon's Congressional Medal of Honor citation says: "For conspicuous gallantry and intrepidity in action at the risk of his life above and beyond the call of duty, Sergeant Lemon [then Sp4c.], Company E, distinguished himself while serving as an assistant machine gunner during the defense of Fire Support Base

Illingworth. When the base came under heavy enemy attack, Sergeant Lemon engaged a numerically superior enemy with machinegun and rifle fire from his defensive position until both weapons malfunctioned. He then used hand grenades to fend off the intensified enemy attack launched in his direction. After eliminating all but one of the enemy soldiers in the immediate vicinity, he pursued and disposed of the remaining soldier in hand-to-hand combat. Despite fragment wounds from an exploding grenade, Sergeant Lemon regained his position, carried a more seriously wounded comrade to an aid station, and, as he returned, was wounded a second time by enemy fire. Disregarding his personal injuries, he moved to his position through a hail of small arms and grenade fire. Sergeant Lemon immediately realized that the defensive sector was in danger of being overrun by the enemy and unhesitatingly assaulted the enemy soldiers by throwing hand grenades and engaging in hand-to-hand combat. He was wounded yet a third time, but his determined efforts successfully drove the enemy from the position. Securing an operable machinegun, Sergeant Lemon stood atop an embankment fully exposed to enemy fire, and placed effective fire upon the enemy until he collapsed from his multiple wounds and exhaustion. After regaining consciousness at the aid station, he refused medical evacuation until his more seriously wounded comrades had been evacuated. Sergeant Lemon's gallantry and extraordinary heroism are in keeping with the highest traditions of the military service and reflect great credit on him, his unit, and the US Army."[10]

So many today still wonder why the United States ultimately spent the lives of more than fifty-eight thousand young American men in the jungles of Southeast Asia in a war that is still argued to be meaningless at a minimum and horrendously insane at its worst. I have read many opinions and arguments about the validity of the Vietnam War. The arguments will never cease … it will be debated endlessly. Although ultimately considered a failure, with communist North Vietnam overtaking its neighbor to the south at a tremendous cost in American lives, many claim the fight for freedom in Southeast Asia was worthwhile. Jack Smith, a veteran of one of the most horrifying battles of the Vietnam conflict who witnessed firsthand the hellish nature of that war, put it about as well as I think I have ever heard or read. His explanation is somewhat lengthy, but here are his exact words. Consider them carefully.

"Whether the war was right or whether it was wrong, it was fought in such a way it could never really have been brought to a conclusion. That now seems clear with time. What a waste. It's why so many veterans of Vietnam feel bitter. Well, we finally did get our parades and we finally did build our memorial on the Mall in Washington. These helped. But so many veterans were still haunted by the war, and I was too. Fourteen years ago I watched the Berlin Wall come down, and as an ABC News correspondent, I witnessed firsthand the collapse of communism. I remember thinking, … *containment worked. We won the Cold War.* And however meaningless Vietnam seemed at the time, it contributed to the fall of communism. Hardly justification for what we went through in Vietnam, but at least it was something.

"Then, ten years ago, an event changed me. An opportunity to go back to Vietnam with ten other Ia Drang veterans, I traveled back to the jungle in the Central Highlands and for several days walked the battlefield. Did I find the answer to my question? No, I don't know if what we did in the war ultimately was worth it. But what I did find surprised me. North Vietnam may have conquered the South, but it is losing the peace. A country that three decades ago had the fourth-strongest army in the world has squandered its wealth on fighting its neighbors and is poor and bankrupt. You look at Vietnam today and you wonder why they fought the war. Many North Vietnamese wonder too. What struck me was the overwhelming peacefulness of the place, even in the clearing where I fought, LZ [landing zone] Albany. I broke down several times. I wanted to bring back some shell casings—some physical manifestation of the battle—to lay at the foot of the Wall here in Washington. But, do you know, search as I did, I could not find any? The forces of nature had simply erased it. And where once the grass had been slippery with blood, there were flowers blooming in that place of death. So I pressed some and brought them back. Flowers ... that's all that I could find in that jungle clearing that once held terror and now held beauty. What I discovered with time may seem obvious, but it had really escaped me all those years on my journey home from Vietnam: the war is over. It certainly is for Vietnam and the Vietnamese people. As I said on a *Nightline* broadcast when I came back, 'This land is at peace, and so should we be.' For me, Vietnam has become a place again, not a war, and I have begun letting go. I have discovered that wounds heal. That the friendship of old comrades breathes meaning into life. And that even the most disjointed events can begin to make sense with the passage of time. This has allowed me, on evenings like this, to step forward and take pride in the service I gave my country. But never to forget what was, and will always be, the worst day of my life. The day I escaped death in the tall grass of the Ia Drang Valley."[11]

After forty-four years, US Army Sergeant Frank Spink has been awarded the Silver Star for his service in Vietnam. The Silver Star is the highest award given by the United States for combat valor. It is given to fewer than one in every two hundred fifty veterans of military service. On the night of June 13, 1968, Sergeant Spink heard enemy movement in the jungles of South Vietnam. After reporting what was to be a major enemy move on the US Special Forces camp in Dak Pek, a village in the Kontum province, a North Vietnamese rocket exploded in Spink's bunker. The attack left Sergeant Spink with a shattered right arm. That right arm was soon to be amputated, but Spink's watchful action helped his Special Forces unit repel the North Vietnamese attack, and his alert actions avoided even heavier losses. Although Sergeant Spink's valor was recognized and written up the following month, a communication foul-up failed to notify him of the honor.

But in March 2012, Spink's old platoon leader, Lt. John McHenry, surprisingly found that Spink had not received his Silver Star. Lieutenant McHenry said, "For all intents and purposes, he has had this medal for the last forty-three years. He was just never made aware of it." Army Sgt. Frank Spink sacrificed by serving his country and doing his duty—losing his arm in the endeavor but most likely saving the lives of many of his Special Forces comrades. He just had to wait forty-four years to receive his recognition.[12]

The Vietnam War, the most unpopular war in the history of the United States, despite its horror, despite the many questions about US diplomacy and aggressive intentions, despite the awful stories of murder and napalm, the Vietnam War still, under its menacing cloud of doubt and conduct, produced unquestionable acts of heroism and sacrifice. So often throughout human history, innocent persons have been placed in tragic and conspicuous circumstances and yet have performed and acted in gallant and remarkable ways to show the best of dedication and loyalty to fellow countrymen and to oppressed peoples throughout the world. And remember, there are thousands of these stories of sacrifice. Do some research. Study them. Remember them.

More importantly, almost forty years after the Vietnam conflict ended, a war that left a terrible footnote on our country's history, we must ask, "What lesson can we now learn?" Like Jack Smith, any of us may someday experience "the worst day of my life." It could be the loss of a job, death of a family member, or a cancer diagnosis. There are many possible scenarios for the worst day of our lives. But like Jack Smith, we can move on from that "worst day" to live better, more committed, more meaningful days. As Americans, we need to remember, appreciate, and thank our Vietnam veterans—not for a questionable and horrible political war but for their gallantry, commitment, service, and sacrifice in the name of freedom. We need to remember within the scope of our freedoms, bought through sacrifice, our role as concerned, committed and responsible citizens of this great nation.

ILLUSTRATION:
TOTAL US MILITARY DEATHS IN ALL US WARS

Total Deaths in Major Wars Fought by the United States

War	Years	Deaths	Deaths/Day
Civil War	1861-65	625,000	599
World War II	1941-45	405,399	416
World War I	1917-18	116,516	279
Vietnam	1964-73	58,151	26
Korean	1950-53	36,516	45
Am. Revolution	1775-83	25,000	11
War of 1812	1812-15	20,000	31
Mexican War	1846-48	13,283	29
Iraq War	2003-2010	4,487	2
Philippine-Am.	1898-1913	4,196	fewer than 1
Spanish-Am.	1898	2,446	5
Afghanistan	2001-present	1,984	fewer than 1

- There have been other American fatalities in international conflicts not listed on the above chart (e.g., the Boxer Rebellion in China in 1900, where 131 Americans lost their lives; the American Expeditionary Force in Siberia from 1918-20, where 613 Americans were killed; various deployments in the 1980s and 1990s [El Salvador, Beirut, Grenada, Panama, Haiti, Kosovo] where well more than one hundred Americans also lost their lives).
- These statistics can be verified by numerous websites by querying "United States casualties of war" in search engines.[13]

Chapter 4

Everyday Heroes

On September 11, 2001, a terrorist attack on the United States of America resulted in the deaths of 2,983 people. Although that never-to-be-forgotten heinous act by terrorist cowards resulting in the collapse of the Twin Towers of the World Trade Center, the crash of American Airlines Flight 77, as well as United Airlines Flight 93 was an episode of American history that counted numerous acts of heroism and sacrifice, I want to concentrate first on the 346 firefighters, police, medical personnel, and rescue workers who sacrificed their lives on that fateful late-summer day. The intended purpose of every one of those heroes was to save the lives of those trapped in the rubble of the Twin Towers and the Pentagon.

As we recollect that fateful Tuesday morning, we need to remember that nineteen al-Qaeda terrorists hijacked four American passenger jet aircraft. American Airlines Flight 11 flying from Boston to Los Angeles and United Airlines Flight 175, also flying from Boston to Los Angeles were hijacked and flown into the World Trade Center Twin Towers. The first jet (American Airlines Flight 11), overtaken by five hijackers, flew into the north tower at 8:46 a.m. Shortly afterward, at 9:03 a.m., another five hijackers, who had taken control of United Flight 175 flew that jet airliner into the south tower. A little more than 30 minutes later, a third airliner, again taken over by five hijackers, flew American Airlines Flight 77, leaving Washington, DC to Los Angeles, into the Pentagon in Arlington, Virginia. Finally, United Airlines Flight 93 flying from Newark, New Jersey, to San Francisco, and under the control of four hijackers, flew over Pennsylvania, most likely headed back to Washington to fly into the Capitol Building or the White House. However, this hijacked flight did not reach its intended target due to the heroic countermeasures of some of the courageous crew and action-oriented passengers. AA Flight 93 crashed in a field near Shanksville, Pennsylvania. There were no survivors from any of the four hijacked aircraft.

The last time anyone saw Richard Rescorla, he was racing up and down stairs at the World Trade Center's south tower, singing "God Bless America" through a bullhorn and calming nerves as he shepherded people to safety. According to his wife, Susan, many survivors have credited Rescorla and his unit for leading them out of the crumbling tower. Morgan Stanley had twenty-seven hundred employees in the World Trade Center; only a dozen or so were lost. Reports from multiple survivors of the south tower told of Rick Rescorla on floors ranging from the tenth to the seventy-second. In fact, at different times, he was on all those floors. Rescorla was ushering employees out of the south tower with a bullhorn, commanding attention and respect as he had done on the battlefield so long ago.[1] You see, Rick Rescorla, director of security for Morgan Stanley at the World Trade Center's south tower, was no stranger to deadly crises and danger. Actually, Rick Rescorla was a battle-tested veteran of Vietnam. What did he do in Vietnam? Remember the Battle of Ia Drang Valley? He was one of the heroes of that battle.

In 1965 Rick risked his very life protecting wounded army buddies fighting off the attacking North Vietnamese. Now in 2011, Rick again was protecting innocent civilians during the worst terrorist attack in US history. As early as 1992 Rescorla warned the Port Authority (owner of the World Trade Center) about the possibility of a truck bomb attack on the pillars in the basement parking garage, but Rescorla's warning was ignored. When terrorists used this method in the 1993 attack, Rescorla was instrumental in evacuating the building, and was the last man out.[2]

Rick Rescorla bravely and valiantly served his country at the Battle of Ia Drang Valley in Vietnam. He died for his country on September 11, 2001, helping save the lives of thousands of people in the World Trade Center south tower.

Twice during her police career, NYPD Officer Moira A. Smith plunged herself into disaster scenes, repeatedly pulling out the maimed and wounded—the first time was on Aug. 27, 1991, a subway crash in Union Square in which five were killed and more than 130 hurt. She was awarded the Police Department's Distinguished Duty Medal for saving dozens of lives and earning the respect of her fellow officers. The second time—the terrorist attack on the WTC—she never made it out.[3] She was the first NYPD Officer to report the first hijacked plane after it hit the north tower. As she assisted with the evacuation of civilians from the north tower, the tower collapsed. The south tower collapsed less than an hour later. Officer Moira A. Smith's remains were found in March 2002. She is survived by her husband, also a NYPD officer, and her now twelve-year-old daughter. Officer Smith was posthumously awarded the New York City Police Department's Medal of Honor for her heroic actions. On September 9, 2005, all the public safety officers killed on September

11, 2001, were posthumously awarded the 9/11 Heroes Medal of Valor by President George W. Bush.[4]

Welles Crowther was a twenty-four year-old investment banker who died on September 11, 2001. But he wasn't a victim. He was a selfless, sacrificial hero. His office was on the 104th floor of the WTC south tower. After American Airlines Flight 175 crashed into the south tower at 9:03 a.m., panic and a feeling of hopelessness engulfed the upper floors. Through the darkness, wreckage, and smoke, Welles Crowther appeared with a red bandana over his mouth and nose and in an authoritative manner assisted people down the stairs to safety. He was seen on three separate occasions reentering the south tower. Crowther helped dozens of people to safety on 9/11. His body was found in March 2002, alongside several firefighters and emergency workers bunched in a suspected command post in the South Tower lobby.[5]

"Mr. Burnett phoned his wife, Deena, four times. In the first call he told her about the situation on the plane and asked her to call authorities. The second time he phoned, he told her he believed their captors were going to fly the plane into the ground. 'The next time he called,' Mrs. Burnett said, 'I could tell they were formulating a plan.' In the last call, he reportedly said, 'I know we're going to die. There's three of us who are going to do something about it.'"[6]

Tom Burnett was described as competitive. After all, there must be some bit of a competitive spirit in someone who led his Minnesota high school team to a semi-state game in 1981. His number 10 jersey has since been retired. But one can understand from his phone calls that day that Tom (and others) were not going to go down without a fight.

Todd Beamer was one of the "others" who is known for his phone conversations with GTE and another operator while on the doomed passenger jet giving information about the hijacking. His most memorable words to his fellow passengers who were going to attempt to thwart the hijackers were, "Let's roll." Todd is survived by his wife, Lisa, their two sons David and Drew, and a daughter, Morgan Kay, born on January 9, 2002, approximately four months after her father's death.[7]

On September 11, 2001, Special Agent Richard Hatton was going to work like any other morning. Special Agent Hatton worked for the FBI. But that morning was different. He saw smoke coming from the north tower of the WTC, so he immediately responded. He then entered one of the towers, helping evacuate victims until the towers fell. He radioed the FBI and relayed what he was witnessing. Special Agent Hatton was forty-five years old and had a wife and four kids. But previously being a volunteer firefighter, he knew he had to do what he could to assist in the disaster. His wife said, "He didn't have to do that, but that was my husband. He joined right in with the fire department to help people and gave his life for it."[8]

Ronald P. Bucca was the only fire marshal in the history of New York City to be killed in the line of duty. His story began like that of every fireman, police officer, and emergency rescue worker on September 11, 2001. At approximately 8:46 a.m., after the impact of the first plane, putting the safety of others before their own, law enforcement officers, along with fire and EMS personnel, rushed to the burning Twin Towers to aid the victims and lead them to safety. Due to the quick actions of NYC's emergency responders, it is estimated that more than twenty-five thousand people were saved that fateful day. Although his actions saved the lives of thousands,

Fire Marshall Bucca continued in his attempt to save lives on the seventy-eighth floor of the south tower when the building collapsed. Bucca was a twenty-two-year veteran of the NYFD having been promoted to fire marshall in 1992. Ron had been a Green Beret in Vietnam. As a fireman in 1986, Ronald Bucca was nicknamed "the Flying Fireman" after he fell spectacularly from a tenement fire escape while fighting a fire, spun around a cable strung through the backyard, and lived to tell the tale. He broke his back in five places. He rehabilitated himself and worked his way back to continue his career as a firefighter.[9] Like 340 other NYC firefighters on September 11, 2001, Fire Marshall Ronald Bucca sacrificed his life in the line of duty, saving thousands of lives.

For Joseph Angelini and his son, Joseph Jr., Hoffman Avenue in Lindenhurst was a familiar road that they traveled almost daily. Every workday they drove it to meet the train that would carry them to their jobs fighting fires as members of the FDNY. Joseph Sr., sixty-three, was the senior member of Brooklyn's Rescue Company 1; his son worked at Manhattan Ladder Company 4. Both were killed when the Twin Towers collapsed. Joseph Angelini was the most veteran firefighter in the city, with forty years on the job. He was tough and "rode the back step" which means he rode the back step of the fire engine like everyone else despite his age. His thirty-eight-year-old son, who worked on Ladder Company 4 on Forty-Eighth Street, had been on the job for seven years.[10] "If he had lived and his son had died, I don't think he would have survived," said Alfred Benjamin, a firefighter at Rescue Company 1 in Manhattan, who was partnered with Mr. Angelini for the last six months.[11]

Father and son, committed public servants who stared death in the face with regularity, died that September morning, perhaps within the same hour, and without a doubt within hours of each other. Often sons follow in their fathers' footsteps … but in this case, Joseph Jr., like his father, died giving his life to save the lives of others. What a family. What a legacy.

Unlike the Angelinis, one son never knew his father because he was born after his firefighter father died September 11.

Patrick Mate Lyons wrote,

"Dear Dad,

I just missed meeting you. You died on September 11, 2001, and I was born twenty-six days later, on October 7. I want you to know that Mommy is doing a great job of loving me and raising me in a happy home. I am almost ten years old now, and from all the stories I've heard about you, I feel like I *do* know you. Every September 11 we go to your firehouse, Squad 252, for a Mass. We get to eat lots of donuts, and see the fire truck. I see it every year … and every year, I think it is so cool.

On your birthday, the Lyons family gets together and we celebrate you. I send a baseball and football balloon up to heaven to make you happy. I think it is really cool that you were such a brave firefighter and that you died saving lots of people's lives. I feel so proud of you. As I get older, *everyone* says I walk like you, run like you, and have your crazy sense of humor too. I play flag football in the same league as you, and in the same position as you, quarterback. In baseball, I pitch, just like you did. I really like it when people compare me to you. Mommy told me that when you found out you were having a boy you wanted me to be a left-handed pitcher in the Majors. Well, here's the thing ... I *bat* lefty, but I *pitch* righty. But I *do* plan to pitch for the New York Mets someday. I have a fun life. Mommy got married again, and I have a dad, a brother, and a sister. My dad plays sports with me and teaches me how to do things like ride a boogie-board, build a sandcastle, build a double-decker birdhouse, and clean the pool. I really love him.

I know that you are in heaven and you are always watching over me. I love knowing that you are a hero. I wish I could have met you.

Love,
Your son, Patrick Mate Lyons"[12]

This letter to a fallen 9/11 firefighter who just happened to have a wife pregnant with their then unborn son was written ten years later by that son who never met his father. Patrick Lyons's father was NYFD Lieutenant Patrick Lyons, who died while saving lives in the collapse of the Twin Towers. Duty and sacrifice. They seem to go together. It is difficult to separate the two concepts. In times of extreme crisis, especially a crisis resulting from catastrophe or disaster, duty and sacrifice may demand extraordinary risk. Risk for the purpose of saving lives may result in death. Giving one's life for the sake of saving the lives of others is the ultimate sacrifice. It is also the ultimate act of love for other human beings.

On September 11, 2001, a total of 411 emergency workers died as they tried to rescue people, clear debris, and fight fires. The New York City Fire Department (FDNY) lost 341 firefighters and two paramedics. The New York City Police Department (NYPD) lost 23 officers. The Port Authority Police Department lost 37 officers. Eight medical technicians (EMTs) and paramedics from private emergency medical services units were killed. Each of those "first responders" had a story. Some were told. Many were not. All were heroes who made the ultimate sacrifice. They did their duty. They gave their lives rescuing those who found themselves caught in the 9/11 disaster. As of August 2011, 1,631 victims have been identified, while 1,122 (41 percent) of the victims remain unidentified. The remains are being held in storage in Memorial Park, outside the New York City medical examiner's facilities. It is expected that the remains will be moved in 2013 to a repository behind a wall at the 9/11 museum. A medical examiner, who will have a workspace at the site, will continue to try to identify remains in the hope improved technology will allow forensic and medical examiners to identify other victims.[13]

Often when we recall September 11, 2001, we think of the senseless loss of thousands of lives. We remember those innocent victims who died at the hands of cowardly terrorists. And we should remember those who died. But at the same time, we need to remember the thousands who live today because of the sacrifices made by police, firefighters, EMTs, and others doing their professional or personal duty on that terrible day.

Since that fateful day, more than eight hundred "first responders" have lost their lives in the line of duty serving and protecting American citizens across this country. According to John 13:15,

"Greater love has no one than this, that he lay down his life for his friends" (NIV).

One of those eight hundred "first responders" was Indianapolis Metropolitan Police Officer David Moore. Officer Moore died on Wednesday, January 26, 2011, from internal injuries suffered from a gunshot wound on Sunday January 23. He was taken immediately to the intensive care unit of Wishard Memorial Hospital after being shot twice in the face and once in the thigh in the 400 block of Temple Avenue in Indianapolis. A forth shot bruised officer Moore's chest, but the bullet did not penetrate due to his protective bulletproof vest. Doctors reported that one of the bullets fractured Officer Moore's spine and another bullet passed through his brain stem and vital blood vessels. Thomas Hardy, sixty, was charged with Moore's shooting on what appeared to be a routine traffic stop. However, Hardy appeared in court also on a robbery charge that occurred within an hour after the shooting of Officer Moore.

David Moore joined the Indianapolis Police Department in 2004 following in the tradition of his parents—both career police officers. David Moore was the IMPD Rookie Officer of the Year in 2005. In 2009 Officer Moore received the Medal of Valor for courage shown in a life-threatening confrontation where Moore shot and killed a man who aimed a gun and him and fellow officers.

Indiana Congressman Andre Carson said of Officer Moore, "There's no doubt Officer Moore knew the dangers of police work, as both of his parents were part of the IMPD family. But like so many who wear the badge in communities across the nation, David Moore took an oath to serve and protect others. To run to danger—not away from it. Officer Moore did just that, and our community is a better and safer place because of his service and sacrifice."[14]

Officer Moore's story is representative of encounters that occur on a daily basis across America, where those sworn to protect and defend the public, to risk and sometimes give their lives carrying out that duty. Why mention Officer David Moore? Because as Americans, we need to remember that police, fire, and other first responders did not just go to work on 9/11 ... they go to work everyday. And they risk their lives in the interest of public safety—our safety—every day, 365 days a year.

But as we all remember, just as that fateful day at Pearl Harbor gave every American a resolve to bring justice to the perpetrators of the attack, a similar, if not greater determination ensued after 9/11. Although December 7, 1941, "a date that will live in infamy" according to FDR, was a terrible day in America's history, we must remember that in 1941, communication was slow. It took days for photographs of what happened in Hawaii to reach the American public. Even then the pictures were generally filtered by the US military. Americans knew lives were lost, but it occurred on an isolated island in the middle of the Pacific. It seemed somewhat distant and removed. But retaliation was sure to come. In the words of Japanese Admiral Isoroku Yamamoto, "I fear all we have done is to awaken a sleeping giant." He was absolutely correct.

The 9/11 attacks, unlike Pearl Harbor, were perpetrated against innocent civilians in peacetime, not military personnel on a war alert status. The 9/11 attacks struck more at the heart of America because they occurred in the middle of populated areas, not against military bases preparing for war. The 9/11 attacks were murderous, killing unsuspecting innocent civilians. And probably most significantly, the events of 9/11 (the aftermath of the first tower strike) and live TV viewing of the second strike were witnessed by millions of Americans as the events happened, bringing about a new kind of "on the scene" witnessing of terrible and devastating events as they transpired. Talk about shock. Talk about anger. Talk about resolve for bringing to justice the cowards who perpetrated such a terrible act.

On that Tuesday evening, September 11, 2001, President George Bush addressed the nation. He appealed personally to every American as he made comments meant to console Americans as well as pledge justice for the terrorists. He said, "The pictures of airplanes flying into buildings, fires burning, huge structures collapsing have filled us with disbelief, terrible sadness, and a quiet, unyielding anger. Terrorist attacks can shake the foundations of our biggest buildings, but they cannot touch the foundation of America. These acts shatter steel, but they cannot dent the steel of American resolve. The search is underway for those who are behind these evil acts. I've directed the full resources for our intelligence and law enforcement communities to find those responsible and bring them to justice. We will make no distinction between the terrorists who committed these acts and those who harbor them."[15]

President Bush's remarks and promises led to a decade long hunt for top al-Qaeda leaders and operatives around the world. The pledge to bring justice to the terrorist organization continues today. Not long ago, on May 1, 2011, not quite ten years since the attacks of 9/11, Osama bin Laden, the undisputed leader of al-Qaeda and one of the masterminds of the 9/11 attacks, was hunted down and killed by a Navy Seal team in Abbottabad, Pakistan. Several other al-Qaeda leaders have been captured or killed in the past decade, but it was the allusiveness of bin Laden that had left a bad taste in the mouths of all Americans. President Barack Obama said of the killing of bin Laden, "Justice has been done." President George W. Bush said, "This momentous achievement marks a victory for America, for people who seek peace around the world, and for those who lost loved ones on September 11, 2001."[16]

We must remember that tracking down this international terrorist just didn't happen, and no one person was responsible for bin Laden's death. Military, intelligence, and political personnel all contributed. After 9/11, the CIA followed leads tracking al-Qaedas' leaders for years. But finally in 2007 the pseudonym identifying a "courier" was linked to a name. After two years of following leads, the location of "courier" and his brother was found in Abbottabad. By September 2010, it was suspected that bin Laden was living at the same location. In March and April 2011, the National Security Council met several times. The final meeting took place on April 28, resulting in President Obama authorizing Seal Team Six to raid the complex where bin Laden was thought to be hiding. After confirmation of the raid and its results, the president appeared on national television stating that US forces had killed bin Laden and had possession of his body. The terrorist's body was placed aboard the USS *Carl Vinson* and given proper burial at sea (North Arabian Sea).[17]

So what does all this have to do with sacrifice? Probably more than we will ever know. The time and effort put into the search for, tracking of, and eventually the killing of this ruthless terrorist and his fellow conspirators is hard to fathom. As the Twin Towers fell into heaps of smoke and ashes, every American wanted justice. Every American was so angry at the perpetrators of this most heinous act of terrorism that they would have done anything to bring the terrorists to justice. America, as a nation, made a commitment after 9/11. A commitment that justice would be served against a terror network that threatened the very security of every American citizen. On May 1, 2011, there was a sense of justice and every American felt it. But it was brought about by the sacrifice of a team of Navy Seals resulting from years of intelligence work.

Navy Seals are the elite of the military elite. Each Seal undergoes a half-year intensive program that only the most mentally astute and physically tough can endure. The first eight-week phase is known as the physical conditioning phase and places a strong emphasis on running, swimming, navigating the obstacle course, and basic water and lifesaving skills. Sounds easy, doesn't it? It's not! This phase pushes the body to its physical and mental limits. Trained medical technicians and instructors are with the students at every step. Complete physical exhaustion is the norm. Extreme temperatures are the norm. Survival is the goal of this ultra-demanding training. Having endured the complexity of First Phase, trainees move on to their next big obstacle—diving. Second Phase is seven weeks in length and emphasizes the skills required to be a Naval Special Warfare combat swimmer. "Third Phase is comparable to First Phase in that you are often cold, miserable, and tired," said Aircrew Survival Equipmentman Second Class Louis G. Fernbough, Third Phase instructor. "The difference is, we now expect you to think and perform mentally under the same conditions. Mistakes made when working with explosives only happen once."[18]

Members of Seal teams, in a fashion similar to firefighters and police officers, understand that they most likely will be put in harm's way when doing their duty. Obviously, the members of Seal Team Six who flew by helicopter into Pakistan unbeknownst to the Pakistani government were on an ultra-secret mission. The possibility of something going wrong existed as it always does in this kind of operation. Actually, one helicopter did crash, but there were no injuries. A high degree of risk was involved.

There is a high degree of risk with every Seal mission. Three months after Osama bin Laden was killed in Pakistan, nearly two dozen Navy Seals in a helicopter were shot down in Afghanistan by Taliban rebels. It was the single largest number of American troops killed in one day since America's military involvement in Afghanistan. "Their deaths are a reminder of the extraordinary sacrifices made by the men and women of our military and their families," President Obama said in a statement just after the tragedy. The President further stated, "We will draw inspiration from their lives, and continue the work of securing our country and standing up for the values that they embodied." Marine General James N. Mattis, commander of U.S. Central Command, said: "We grieve for our lost comrades and especially for their families, yet we also remember that the lads were doing what they wanted to be doing and they knew what they were about. This loss will only make the rest of us more determined, something that may be difficult for those who aren't in the military to understand."[19]

But the real nature of risk and sacrifice are not just limited to Navy Seals. They go hand in hand with combat troops on the ground in Afghanistan as well. On September 8, 2009, Marine Corporal Dakota Meyer killed eight Taliban militants and saved the lives of thirteen US soldiers and twenty-three Afghan soldiers. Corporal Meyer and another Marine, Sergeant Rodriquez, listening by radio from a support position, realized their marine comrades were under attack, more like an ambush, from approximately fifty Taliban militants. Five American troops and nine Afghan soldiers died in the ambush, along with many of the fifty insurgents who waged the assault. But it was the actions of Corporal Meyer and Sergeant Rodriquez that also deserve recognition. Coming across some wounded allied Afghan fighters, the pair brought them to safety and headed back in. In all, the duo entered the battle zone five times, rescuing twenty-three Afghans and thirteen Americans. They also extracted the bodies of four Americans who had been killed in the fighting.[20]

Corporal Meyer was recently awarded the Congressional Medal of Honor for his bravery. President Obama noted that Meyer was being honored just days after the tenth anniversary of the September 11 terrorist attacks that prompted the United States to engage in the war. The Obama administration had previously awarded the Medal of Honor to two other Afghan war veterans. Army Staff Sgt. Salvatore Giunta, who received the award November 27, 2010, and Sgt. First Class Leroy Petry, who was awarded the medal at a White House ceremony last month, are the only other living service members given the honor for actions in combat after September 11. Meyer is the second marine to receive the medal for heroism in Iraq or Afghanistan. Previously, Cpl. Jason Dunham was awarded the medal posthumously for throwing his body on a grenade to save fellow marines. Corporal Dunham, while manning a checkpoint in Karabilah, Iraq, was attacked by an Iraqi insurgent carrying a hand grenade. As two marines approached to assist Dunham, the grenade fell from the insurgent's hand. Corporal Dunham dropped to the ground to cover the grenade with his body, saving the lives of his fellow marines.[21] Corporal Dunham made the ultimate sacrifice and saved the lives of his comrades-in-arms in doing so.

In Iraq (OPERATION IRAQI FREEDOM) and Afghanistan (OPERATION ENDURING FREEDOM), America has lost more than six thousand soldiers.[22] They all sacrificed their lives serving the

United States of America in a worldwide campaign to stop terrorism and ultimately establish a safety net that would hopefully prevent future 9/11s. Freedom from terror is bought with a very high price. The price can only be defined one way—sacrifice.

As a side note, there is evidence that some American atrocities have occurred during these wars. Atrocities have occurred in every war in history. That is no excuse for Americans to commit these acts. Atrocities by definition are always violent, brutal and, completely atrocious—thus the name. However, these actions should be dealt with in the form of military courts and punishments and should in no way take away from the acts of valor and sacrifice that have been exemplified by those who have risked and given their lives in the cause of human freedom.

As normal, everyday citizens, living in what appears to be a safe and secure environment, we often overlook the real nature of the world. The world is a dangerous place, where the evil intents of our enemies are often much closer than we might realize. The actual war that began with the 9/11 tragedy still goes on today. The most recent terrorist attack on our embassy in Benghazi, Libya, is a prime example. Our ambassador and three other US diplomatic aides were brutally killed by Middle Eastern terrorists, probably linked to al-Qaeda. And terrorist groups like al-Qaeda threaten our government's diplomats, embassies, and property around the world. Although we often put the thought out of our mind, there are real enemies within our borders as well as beyond our shores that wish to destroy the United States and bring harm or death to its citizens.

What should we learn from 9/11, Iraq, Afghanistan, and other world hot-spots, where terrorist organizations plot to harm the United States and its citizens? Surely we have learned that we are truly at war, and like it or not, we should count our blessings for our freedoms and for those in the military and intelligence areas of our government who watch day and night to protect us. As American citizens, we surely can see the sacrifices that have been made and continue to be made daily to protect and defend our borders, even if those sacrifices are made halfway around the world or right here on our own soil. There are many ways to show support and offer thanks for our military and government officials who wage this war on terrorism. If you have no idea what you can do, go to the Wounded Warrior website www.woundedwarriorproject.org and you will find some ideas. What can you do to show your support and gratitude to those who make our country safe and free?

Chapter 5

A Different Form of Sacrifice

Then Jesus came to them and said, "All authority in heaven and on earth has been given to me. Therefore go and make disciples of all nations, baptizing them in the name of the Father and of the Son, and of the Holy Spirit, and teaching them to obey everything I have commanded you. And surely I am with you always, to the very end of the age."

—Matthew 26:18-20 (NIV)

Throughout the annals of Christianity, it would be impossible to estimate the number of believers who have given their lives in the name of Christ and for his kingdom. In the last hours before Christ's crucifixion, Jesus said to Pontius Pilate, "My kingdom is not of this world ..." Pilate was the fifth prefect of the Roman province of Judea, the judge at the Roman trial of Jesus and answerable only to Tiberius, the emperor of Rome, when it came to all governmental matters in Judea. Pilate certainly had worldly power. But Jesus, the creator of all things and omnipotent in all ways, was not about worldly power. His kingdom was not of this world.

Starting with the stoning of Stephen to modern-day missionary martyrs like Nate Saint in the jungles of Ecuador, Christian missionaries and followers of Christ have put their lives on the line following the Great Commission of Matthew 28:19-20. *Fox's Book of Martyrs* should be required reading for anyone who professes Christ as his or her Savior and Lord. The book, written by John Fox, is a history of the lives, sufferings, and deaths of early Christian martyrs.

John Fox was born at Boston in Lincolnshire, England in 1517. A scholar, he entered Oxford at age sixteen. Fox resigned from his college in 1545 after becoming an evangelical and thereby subscribing to beliefs condemned by the Church of England under Henry VIII. In his book, Fox presents crucial evidence and tells one side of a story that must be heard. Fox gives accounts of Christian martyrs from Stephen through the mid-sixteenth century. Others have continued his work chronicling the deaths of Christian martyrs to the present day.

Stephen, according to Acts 6:5, was "a man full of faith and of the Holy Spirit." Acts 6:8 also records, "Now Stephen, a man full of God's grace and power, did great wonders and miraculous signs among the people." Stephen preached the gospel of Christ to the betrayers and murderers of Christ. The mob became crazed, cast Stephen out of Jerusalem and stoned him. "And Saul [Paul, the future apostle] was there giving approval to his death" (Acts 8:1, NIV).

The persecution against the church continued after Stephen's stoning. It was a great persecution according to the book of Acts, scattering the church throughout the regions of Judea and Samaria except for the apostles. The apostles continued preaching the resurrection of Jesus, knowing their lives were in grave danger.

James, the son of Zebedee, the elder brother of John and relative of Jesus, was the next martyr in the chronology of the apostles' deaths. He was sometimes referred to as James the Great. A full decade after the death of Stephen, when Herod Agrippa raised a violent persecution against the church, the king decided to strike hardest at the leaders of the Christian movement. About 44 AD, in an account given to us by the Greek theologian Clemens Alexandrinus, the apostle James was led to his place of martyrdom, where he was beheaded. Ironically, the accuser of James, repenting of his conduct and inspired by James's extraordinary courage and faith, professed himself a Christian and was beheaded alongside the apostle. So the first of the twelve disciples of Christ bravely and cheerfully drank from the bitter cup that he told Christ he was ready to drink.[1]

On July 27, 2011, the Turkish news agency Anadolu reported that archeologists had unearthed the tomb of Saint Philip during excavations in Hierapolis, close to the Turkish city Denizli. The Italian professor Francesco D'Andria stated that scientists had discovered the tomb within a newly revealed church. He stated that the design of the tomb, and writings on its walls, definitively prove it belonged to the martyred apostle of Jesus.[2]

Philip was a disciple of Jesus, according to the gospel of John and is mentioned most often in that gospel account. Philip bore a Greek name and probably spoke the language. It was Philip who introduced members of the Greek community to Jesus at the Passover Feast upon Christ's triumphal entry into Jerusalem one week before his crucifixion. Philip's entry in *Fox's Book of Martyrs* says, "Was born at Bethsaida, in Galilee, and was first called by the name of 'disciple.' He was martyred in Heliopolis, in Phrygia. He was scourged, thrown into prison, and afterward crucified." Fox places Philip's death in 54 AD. Other sources have placed his martyrdom as late as 80 AD.

The apostle Matthew, also called Levi, a Jew of Galilee, was originally a tax collector under the employ of the Roman Empire who became one of the twelve apostles and the author of the first gospel. He was the son of Alphaeus, born at Capernaum, a settlement on the shore of the Sea of Galilee, about a year after the birth of Jesus. Through his work as a tax collector, Matthew gained knowledge of languages such as Aramaic, Greek, and Hebrew. The Roman system for collecting taxes lent itself to fraud and corruption. Wealthy people would "bid" on the right to collect taxes in their region. Anything a tax gatherer collected in excess of the Roman government's demands was kept as profit. Tax collectors were considered "unclean" because according to Jewish law, they had unacceptable forms of contact with Gentile people (the Romans as well as other cultures). Tax collectors were also commonly regarded as thieves because they were often fraudulent and dishonest, charging extortionist amounts of taxes due to the intimidation of the Roman tax collection system.[3]

Matthew's call to become a disciple of Jesus was simple according to Matthew 9:9, which says, "As Jesus went on from there, he saw a man, named Matthew sitting at the tax collector's booth. 'Follow me,' he told him, and Matthew got up and followed him" (NIV). Matthew wrote his gospel account in the Hebrew language, which was then translated into Greek by the apostle James. Matthew's missionary labors were in Parthia and Ethiopia. He suffered martyrdom in Nadabah, Ethiopia, in AD 60.[4]

The next apostle to be martyred was James (the Less), not to be confused with the earlier James (the Great). James (also sometimes referred to as James the Just), was the author of the New Testament book of James. James was noteworthy due to his selection to the oversight of the churches of Jerusalem. Paul mentioned James, as well as Cephas and John, as pillars in the church at Jerusalem (Galatians

2:9). According to Acts 21:18-24, James was said to be a religious man, austere, legal, and ceremonial. It was James who presided over the first counsel of apostles and elders in Jerusalem mentioned in Acts 15. According to a passage in Josephus's *Antiquities of the Jews* (xx. 9), "the brother of Jesus, who was called Christ, whose name was James" met his death after the death of the procurator Porcius Festus, yet before Lucceius Albinus took office (*Antiquities* 20,9)—which has thus been dated to AD 62. At the age of ninety-four, he (James) was beaten and stoned by the Jews and finally had his brains dashed out with a fuller's club.[5]

"Then Satan entered Judas, called Iscariot, one of the Twelve. And Judas went to the chief priests and the officers of the temple guard and discussed with them how he might betray Jesus" (Luke 22:3-4, NIV). "When Judas, who had betrayed him, saw that Jesus was condemned, he was seized with great remorse and returned the thirty pieces of silver coins to the chief priests and the elders. 'I have sinned,' he said, 'for I have betrayed innocent blood'" (Matthew 27:3-4, NIV). Since one of the twelve had now committed suicide after his betrayal of Christ, the remaining disciples looked for a replacement. The lot fell to a man named Matthias. There is less known about Matthias than the other disciples. However, it is known that Matthias was a follower of Christ from the time of Jesus' baptism through to his death and resurrection, and likely one of the seventy-two sent out to preach and heal. Matthias was chosen by prayer and the drawing of lots to replace Judas Iscariot as the twelfth apostle (Acts 1:15-28, NIV).

No more is heard about him in the New Testament, and the various traditions are made more confusing because of the similarity of his name to Matthew's. However, according to *Fox's Book of Martyrs*, Matthias was "stoned at Jerusalem and then beheaded."

Most references to Andrew in the New Testament simply include him as part of the twelve apostles, or include him in the same sentence as his brother, Simon Peter. But Andrew acted alone on three separate occasions in the gospel of John. When a number of Greeks desired an audience with Jesus, they came to Philip, who then told Andrew, and together the two of them told Jesus (John 12:20-22). Before Jesus fed the five thousand, it was Andrew who said, "Here is a boy with five small barley loaves and two small fish" (John 6:8f. NIV). And the first two disciples whom John reported as attaching themselves to Jesus (John 1:35-42) are Andrew and another disciple whom John did not name, but who was most likely John himself. Having met Jesus, Andrew then sought out his brother Simon and brought him to meet Jesus. Thus, on each occasion when he was mentioned as an individual, it was because he was instrumental in bringing others to meet the Lord. Andrew preached the gospel to many Asiatic nations, but on his arrival at Edessa (modern-day southeastern Turkey) he was taken and crucified on a cross, the two ends of which were fixed transversely in the ground. Hence the derivation of the name St. Andrew's Cross.[6]

"John, also called Mark" (Acts 12:12), like some of other apostles and disciples, was known by different names. He was one of the seventy-two disciples sent out by Jesus in Luke 10:1-23. Mark (Marcus) was his Roman name, and John was his Hebrew name. He is called John in Acts 13:5 and 13. He is called Mark in Acts 15:39 and 2 Timothy 4:11. His Roman name was used as the title of his gospel, probably to avoid the confusion of having two gospel books with the same name. It is likely Mark was born near Jerusalem where his mother lived during the New Testament time. There is no record of his father but Mark is described as a cousin of Barnabas (Colossians 4:10). Mark's mother's house was apparently a popular place for Christians to assemble, "where many people had gathered and were praying" (Acts 12:12, NIV). Peter went to her house immediately after an angel sprang him from Herod's prison (Acts 12:6-12). Peter refers to Mark as "my son" in 1 Peter 5:13 (NIV), so it is likely that Peter was involved in Mark's conversion. Peter would have been in his mid-30s at that time and Mark was substantially younger. Peter was definitely a mentor to Mark. There is speculation that Peter was actually Mark's biological father, although there is nothing specific written in the Bible that would validate that conclusion. We do know Peter was married (1 Corinthians 9:5), but his wife's name is not known.

The "young man" spoken of in Mark 14:51-52 was, most likely, Mark himself. He is first mentioned by name in Chapter 12 of Acts. Mark accompanied Paul and Barnabas on their first missionary journey but for some reason returned to Jerusalem after they had journeyed as far as Perga in Pamphylia (Acts 12:25; 13:13). It was this first missionary journey that later caused a "sharp disagreement" between Paul and Barnabas. Paul then refused to take Mark with him on another missionary journey because of the disagreement (Acts 15:36-40). They did, however, reconcile at a later time because Mark was with Paul in his first imprisonment at Rome (Colossians 4:10, Philemon 1:24). At a later time, Mark was with Peter (1 Peter 5:13) and then with Timothy in Ephesus (2 Timothy 4:11). Mark then disappears from the record. Mark was one of the fortunate few to have seen and heard Jesus Christ during His human lifetime. It is said that Mark was "dragged to pieces by the people of Alexandria, at the great solemnity of Serapis their idol, ending his life under their merciless hands."[7]

The apostle Peter may have been, according to the gospels, the most prominent of the disciples. Peter was born in Bethsaida, Galilee. He was a fisherman, as was his father and brother, the apostle Andrew. Peter and Andrew, along with their friends and fishing business associates, the apostles James and John, did their fishing on the Sea of Galilee. After meeting Jesus and following his ministry, Peter began to believe Jesus was the Messiah due to Christ's miracles, teachings, and acts of love and compassion. Peter's faith was so strong that Jesus gave him the name Cephas (the rock). Peter is actually the Greek translation of Cephas.

It was Peter who preached to the masses in Jerusalem on the day of Pentecost (following Jesus' ascension to heaven.) His message is recorded in the New Testament of the Bible, the book of Acts, Chapter 2. Peter is also the one who prompted the disciples to choose a replacement to take over the apostolic ministry of Judas Iscariot (after Judas' betrayal of Jesus.) It was Peter who healed a man who was more than forty years of age and who had been crippled from birth with but the words, "Silver and gold I do not have, but what I have I give to you. In the name of Jesus Christ of Nazareth, walk" (Acts 3:6-7, NIV). Peter was called by the apostle Paul a "pillar" of the Church. It was also believed by the crowds that the mere casting of his shadow upon the sick was capable of bringing about miraculous healing. Peter is the one who defended the inclusion of the Gentiles (non-Jews) into the Christian Church at the Apostolic Council in Jerusalem. His ministry was primarily to the Jews, as the apostle Paul's was to the Gentiles.[8]

After being imprisoned multiple times in Jerusalem because of his faith, Peter left with his wife and possibly others. It is believed he ministered in Babylon to the Jewish colonists there. It is also believed to be in this location where he wrote his first epistle (1 Peter.) Peter eventually went to Rome. While there, it is believed that John Mark, the writer of the gospel of Mark, served as his translator as he preached.[9]

In separate historical writings, the earliest mention that we have of Peter's death is in a letter from Clement, bishop of Rome (AD 88-97), to the Corinthians. He mentions the suffering and martyrdom of Peter and Paul in Rome. Dionysius, bishop of Corinth, makes the following testimony (around 180 AD) writing about Peter and Paul: "Both of these having planted the church at Corinth, likewise instructed us; and having in like manner taught in Italy, they suffered martyrdom about the same time." About twenty years later, Tertullian, a Christian teacher, mentions the martyrdom of Peter and Paul as occurring in Rome under Nero. Peter's death is also recorded by Caius, an ecclesiastical writer (third century), who states that Peter and Paul "suffered martyrdom about the same time." Eusebius, in his book *Ecclesiastical History* (AD 325), says, "Thus Nero publicly announcing himself as the chief enemy of God was led on in his fury to slaughter the apostles. It is said that Paul was beheaded at Rome, and Peter to have been crucified under him. This account is confirmed by the fact that the names of Peter and Paul still remain in the cemeteries of that city even to this day" (*Ecclesiastical History* 2:25).[10]

According to John Fox, "Jerome saith that he was crucified, his head being down and his feet upward, himself so requiring, because he was (he said) unworthy to be crucified after the same form and manner as the Lord was." Jerome was a fourth-century historian born in Dalmatia (modern-day Slovenia). He was educated in Rome.[11] Jerome was probably the greatest Christian scholar in the world by his mid-30s. Perhaps the greatest figure in the history of Bible translation, he spent three decades creating a Latin version that would be the standard for more than a millennium.[12]

Paul, as just mentioned along with Peter, suffered under the persecution of the emperor Nero. Originally known as Saul of Tarsus, he was one of the greatest persecutors of early Christians and the first-century church. Saul met Christ on the road to Damascus. While traveling from Jerusalem to Damascus on a mission to "bring [Christians] which were there bound unto Jerusalem," the resurrected Jesus appeared to him in a great light. Saul was struck blind, but after three days his sight was restored by Ananias of Damascus, and Paul began to preach that Jesus of Nazareth is the Jewish Messiah and the Son of God. Paul became the primary missionary unto the Gentiles. His three missionary journeys took him to Asia Minor, around the Mediterranean, and to Galatia and Phrygia. The message of a risen Christ and Savior was aggravating for Jews as well as many pagan believers. During his first missionary journey, Paul was stoned in the city of Lystra for healing a crippled man. Some Jews dragged him out of the city thinking he was dead, but when his disciples came around him, he miraculously got up and went into the city.[13] Paul was also put in prison while he was in Philippi and also in Jerusalem. According to *Fox's Book of Martyrs,* Paul was beheaded in Rome sometime in the mid-60s AD. Nero ruled Rome until 68 AD when, facing assassination, the insane Roman emperor committed suicide.

All the apostles, except John, met a terrible death. Jude, also known as Thaddeus, the brother of James, was crucified at Edessa in AD 72.[14] Bartholomew preached in many countries and translated the gospel of Matthew into the Indian language. He was cruelly beaten and crucified in Armenia (modern-day Turkey).[15] Other traditions say he was beheaded, but most accounts indicate he was flayed alive and then crucified upside down.[16] Thomas, the one who doubted Jesus had risen from the dead until he could see the nail prints in his hands, preached the gospel in Parthia and India, where after inciting the rage of pagan priests, was martyred by being thrust through with a spear.[17]

Luke, author of the gospel of the same name, was a traveling companion of Paul's. Luke's writings are the single largest contribution to the New Testament. His written gospel is the longest book in the New Testament; when we add his second volume, the Acts of the apostles, we have more than one-quarter of the length of the New Testament writings. Luke wrote excellent Greek; in fact, his Greek is the best in all of Scripture.[18] He was a physician who lived in Antioch, and according to *Fox's Book of Martyrs*, early legends say he was hanged from an olive tree by idolatrous priests in Greece.

There is very little known for sure about the apostle Simon, surnamed Zelotes. Church traditions state Simon is often associated with Jude as an evangelizing team; they share their feast day on October 28. The most widespread tradition is that after evangelizing in Egypt, Simon joined Jude in Persia and Armenia, where both were martyred.[19] However, *Fox's Book of Martyrs* states that Simon was crucified in Britain in AD 74.

Fox's book also records that the death of the apostle Barnabas took place around AD 73. Barnabas is most often associated with the apostle Paul. His story is told in Acts. Barnabas is also mentioned in the apostle Paul's writings. Church tradition describes the martyrdom of many saints, including the story of the martyrdom of Barnabas. It relates that certain Jews coming to Syria and Salamis, where Barnabas was then preaching the gospel, being highly exasperated at his extraordinary success, fell upon him as he was disputing in the synagogue, dragged him out, and, after the most inhumane tortures, stoned him to death. His kinsman, John Mark, who was a spectator of this barbarous action, privately interred his body.[20]

The apostle John, author of the gospel of John, was also known in scriptural accounts as "the disciple whom Jesus loved," or perhaps better translated "The Beloved Disciple." After Jesus' ascension and the descent of the Holy Spirit on the Day of Pentecost, John, together with Peter, took a prominent part in the founding and guidance of the church. He was with Peter at the healing of the lame man in the temple. He was also thrown into prison with Peter and was with Peter visiting the newly converted in Samaria.[21]

John was the brother of James (the Great). The churches of Smyrna, Pergamos, Sardis, Philadelphia, Laodicea, and Thyatira were founded by John. "From Ephesus John was ordered to be sent to Rome, where it is affirmed he was cast into a cauldron of boiling oil. He escaped by miracle, without injury."[22]

The emperor Domitian exiled John to the Isle of Patmos. It was there that John wrote the final book of the Bible, Revelation. As far as we know, John was the only disciple to have escaped a violent death.

Fox's Book of Martyrs contains the accounts of literally hundreds of early Christian church martyrs. The subsequent deaths of all those who have sacrificed their lives for the kingdom of Christ are no less important than the deaths of the original twelve apostles or any of the other early Christians mentioned previously. The important point is that their faith in Christ and His coming kingdom was more important to them than earthly life itself. They sacrificed their lives in much the same way that Christ sacrificed his—telling a lost world of God's great love for mankind and his "Good News" message of a Savior who would be "pierced for our transgressions" according to Isaiah 53:5. Isaiah continues in the fifty-third chapter by saying of the Messiah, "he was crushed for our iniquities; the punishment that brought us peace was upon him; and by his wounds we are healed" (Isaiah 53:5, NIV).

Christian martyrs throughout the centuries maintained a steadfast and abiding faith in the Son of God who, according to the apostle Paul in Romans 8:17, made them "heirs of God, and co-heirs with Christ" (NIV). Those martyrs, along with Paul, believed, "I consider that our present sufferings are not worth comparing with the glory that will be revealed in us" (Romans 8:18, NIV). Thousands, more likely millions of Christians from the early days of church history to the present age, have literally risked their lives for either the spreading of the gospel of Christ or for other Christians (and I'm sure non-Christians also) who were facing perilous circumstances. Paul mentions Aquila and Priscilla in his letter to the Romans. "They risked their lives for me" (Romans 16:4, NIV). They, like Paul, believed, "For I am convinced that neither death nor life, neither angels nor demons, neither the present nor the future, nor any powers, neither height nor depth, nor anything else in all creation, will be able to separate us from the love of God that is in Christ Jesus our Lord" (Romans 8:38-39, NIV).

Christian martyrdom has been a constant since the days Jesus walked the earth. Understand, as stated earlier, to even begin to list or enumerate those who have been martyred in the name of Christ would be impossible. Without question, the numbers are in the millions. But to give one example, in one singular period of world history, is appropriate. The persecution of Christians during the days of the Roman Empire is well-known. The most extreme persecutions occurred over a period of about three centuries under the emperors Nero, Domitian, Trajan, Marcus Aurelius, Septimus Severus, Maximinus the Thracian, Decius, Valerian, Diocletian and Galerius, and finally under Julian. Although Constantine became emperor in 306 AD, and he did much to make Christianity an accepted religion, the persecutions did not end there. All in all, these persecutions began just a few years after the death and resurrection of Jesus and lasted approximately three hundred years until about 361 AD (Julian). Christian persecutions continued in the Roman Empire to a greater or lesser degree through the fifth century. Although no one knows the number of Christians martyred under Roman despotism, to estimate that the figure numbers well into the multiple thousands would be a gross underestimation. A more accurate estimation would be hundreds of thousands if not millions.

Put all this in the perspective of time. Christian persecution and martyrdom under Rome lasted about five hundred years. It has now been two thousand years since Christ walked the earth, and the persecution and martyrdom of Christians did not stop with the fall of Rome. It has continued until the present day. Although we cannot find the martyrdom of Christians in our modern world on the scale of the Roman Empire, Christian persecution and martyrdom still occurs today. According to the website, www.christianity.about. com, the average number of Christians martyred for their faith in our modern-day world, is about 160,000 each year. The persecution and execution of Christians in dictatorships (communist, fascist, and other forms of despotism) around the world in this century alone is well documented. Under the regimes of Stalin, Hitler, Mussolini,

Tojo, Mao Zedong, and many, many more, Christians have been persecuted and executed. Most Communist regimes have found Christians to be an easy target.

One current-day example is that of Youcef Nadarkhani, a Christian who recently suffered in prison and was awaiting a death sentence from the Iranian government because he refused to deny Jesus Christ and convert to Islam. In a report by Dan Merica of CNN on September 30, 2011, Merica said, "Nadarkhani, the leader of a network of house churches in Iran, was first convicted of apostasy in November 2010, a charge he subsequently appealed all the way to the Iranian Supreme Court. After four days of an appeals trial that started on a Sunday at a lower court in Gilan Province, Nadarkhani refused to recant his beliefs. Secretary of State Hillary Clinton released a statement the following Friday that said the United States stands with 'all Iranians against the Iranian government's hypocritical statements and actions.' The White House released a statement on the following Thursday stating Nadarkhani 'has done nothing more than maintain his devout faith, which is a universal right for people.'" Perhaps due to the growing international criticism and protest, the Iranian government recently set Nadarkhani free.[23]

In Iran, as well as most Middle Eastern Islamic nations, Sharia law is the law of the land. Sharia law is strict Islamic law. Unlike democratic nations where citizens are free to choose their religion and practice it in privacy protected by law, nations such as Iran do not tolerate any religion other than Islam. Youcef Nadarkhani violated strict Islamic laws by choosing another religion, Christianity. In Iran and other Islamic nations who practice it, Sharia law continually wages war against all other religions, especially the gospel of Christ. In the case of Youcef Nadarkhani, one can easily surmise that originally the Iranian government trumped up multiple charges against him. But the true reason for his imprisonment and at one point, his potential execution, was that he refused to deny Christ as his Savior and Lord.

While watching the October 9, 2011, telecast of CBS's *60 Minutes*, an example of Christian oppression was aired in the segment covering the state of Egypt since the overthrow and resignation of Egyptian President Hosni Mubarak in February 2011. The CBS video scene showed a number, perhaps ten or fifteen Egyptian soldiers in the streets of Cairo beating, kicking, and generally attacking a Coptic Christian.[24] Coptic Christians, often referred to as *Copts*, are simply Egyptian Christians. The Copts were protesting the burning down of a church and what they claim was a pattern of government discrimination against Christians when they clashed with Egyptian security forces. The Christian protesters, led by several Christian church bishops, burned photos of Mostafa el-Sayed, the governor of Aswan province where the Coptic Church was destroyed. The Coptic Church was attacked on September 30 after el-Sayed said the Copts built it without permission. Thousands of Coptic Christians marched, demanding the governor step down and the church be rebuilt. Protesters said it was a peaceful march but they came under attack by government-paid thugs who hit them with stones. "Thugs attacked us, and a military vehicle jumped over a sidewalk and ran over at least ten people. I saw them," protester Essam Khalili, wearing a white shirt with a cross on it, told the reporter from the *Associated Press*.[25]

One final example of modern-day persecution that has generated significant notice within the Christian community as well as throughout the world press in general is the case of Alimujiang Yimiti. Yimiti, a Uyghur Christian and convert from Islam and father of two children, was issued a notice in September 2007 by the Kashgar Xinjiang Ministry of Ethnic and Religious Affairs of China, accusing him of spreading Christianity in the Kashgar area. On January 11, 2008, he was arrested by Kashgar public security officers. He remained incarcerated with no verdict for almost two years. On November 25, 2009, the Kashgar Intermediate Court harshly convicted him on the fabricated charge of "illegally providing state secrets to overseas organizations," giving him the maximum sentence of fifteen years in prison and five years deprivation of his political rights. The verdict was stamped August 6, 2009, but was not received by Alim's lawyer Li Dunyong until December 7.[26] Being kept in what most would call isolation, and after multiple appeals for visitation, on April 20, 2010, Alim's mother, his wife, and his two sons saw him for the first time in more than two years. His mother encouraged her son to be strong, and Alimujiang in turn comforted his family, not knowing when he would see them again. His mother and wife continue to work for his release and urge the international community to demand his release.[27]

But the case of Alimujiang Yimiti is not an isolated incident in China. In continuing religious freedom violations, the Chinese government placed five hundred members of a Protestant church under house arrest between the fall of 2010 and the fall of 2011, according to a Congress-mandated report on China released in 2011. As of April 29, 2012, all seven pastors of the church were still in custody. On May 10, 2012, the report records, public security officials in Zhengzhou city interrupted a Chinese House Church Alliance (CHCA) Bible study and took forty-nine people into custody.[28]

In all truth, the fact is that times have not changed much in two thousand years. Just like the original apostles who lived out their faith and preached the gospel of Christ, millions of Christians around the world today are currently suffering persecution for their faith. Most often persecution takes the form of imprisonment, abuse, and civil as well as political hostilities. But in some cases, just like the apostles, Christians are asked to face more than scorn, incarceration, or the loss of wealth and health—they are asked to face death.

As free Americans, when we read about the persecution of Christians in hostile governments around the world, we must keep in mind the basis for the greatness of the United States of America. We are a nation with citizens who have individual rights. "We hold these truths to be self-evident, that all men are created equal, that they are endowed by their Creator with certain unalienable Rights, that among these are Life, Liberty and the pursuit of Happiness.— That to secure these rights, Governments are instituted among Men, deriving their just powers from the consent of the governed ..."

We all recognize these bold and powerful words from the Declaration of Independence. Abraham Lincoln reemphasized, paraphrased, or at least put the concepts into different words in his Gettysburg address, "And that government of the people, by the people, for the people shall not perish from the earth." The basis of our government is individual liberty within a system of government whose power comes from the people. Thank God for our liberty and individual freedoms. But also remember that these freedoms were bought with a price—the price of sacrifice. All the more, as a free people, we need to be watchful that these precious freedoms are not taken for granted or for any number of reasons placed in jeopardy.

For today's Christian, in the chaos of the world's tumultuous political scene, it is important to distinguish between worldly political rights (or the lack thereof)—those political rights that are granted by world governments—and the God-given rights that are spiritual in nature. I think the apostles and early Christians as well as those Christians who have been persecuted throughout history had to make this same distinction. To put it simply, any government that can give rights to its people can also take those political rights from its people.

The pages of history are fraught with examples of this kind of political power play, which usually transpires at the hands of megalomaniacs backed by military power most often in times of economic and social upheaval. The freedom that we find in God's Word is not of this world. Jesus said, "Then you will know the truth, and the truth will set you free" (John 8:31, NIV). What Jesus was talking about was a spiritual freedom that only comes through a personal, saving relationship with Jesus Himself. Like the apostles and millions of other Christians since the time of Christ, we know there is only one name under heaven by which man can be saved to experience the ultimate eternal freedom prepared for those who love and serve God. The one name is that of the risen Savior, Jesus Christ.

Consider the following Scriptures and then determine your priorities regarding political rights (rights that can be taken away by the power of government) and your spiritual rights as God has ordained them in his Word (spiritual rights that cannot be taken away by man).

- John 8:32—"Then you will know the truth, and the truth will set you free."
- John 8:36—"So if the Son sets you free, you will be free indeed."
- Romans 6:18—"You have been set free from sin and have become slaves to righteousness."

- Romans 6:22—"But now that you have been set free from sin and have become slaves of God, the benefit you reap leads to holiness, and the result is eternal life."
- Romans 8:2—"because through Christ Jesus the law of the Spirit who gives life has set you free from the law of sin and death."
- Galatians 5:1—"It is for freedom that Christ has set us free. Stand firm, then, and do not let yourselves be burdened by a yoke of slavery."

Chapter 6

Closer to Home

This chapter may be the most difficult for me to write. And then, it may be the easiest. There will be few footnotes for this chapter. I grew up in a small town in central Indiana. As I have told my own children, I grew up in Mayberry. I really grew up in Greenwood, Indiana, but it was a lot like Mayberry on the *Andy Griffith Show*. It was a small town with about ten thousand or fifteen thousand people. It seemed everyone knew everyone else. Schools were small. Parents knew the teachers. My high school senior class numbered a whopping 128.

To this day, and I'm sixty-two years old, three of my high school classmates and I meet for a few days each summer to check off another item on our "bucket list." For three or fours days during August 2010, my high school buddies and I traveled to New York to visit the Baseball Hall of Fame in Cooperstown, and Massachusetts to visit the Basketball Hall of Fame in Springfield and to take in a Red Sox game at Fenway Park and its "green monster." We also enjoyed the "Freedom Walk" in downtown Boston. For a few more days in August 2011, we traveled to Kentucky and Tennessee visiting minor league baseball games and playing golf.

In June of 2012 we traveled to Omaha, Nebraska, to watch the college baseball world series. In future years we have plans on the drawing board ... the Masters, the Robert Trent Jones Golf Trail, and who knows, maybe even a World Series or Super Bowl game. The great thing about this is that the four of us grew up in the same small town, played little league baseball and high school sports together, and we have a multitude of great memories that continue to bring us back together. We have been lifelong friends, and occasionally, when no one is listening, we'll utter those very meaningful words, "I love you guys," just like Coach Norman Dale (Gene Hackman) did in the movie *Hoosiers*.

My high school friends and I have many commonalities because our past links us. Obviously when we graduated high school, we set out on our own paths seeking our destinies. And, thankfully, we were all successful in our quest to be solid contributors to American society. We all found good jobs. We all married wonderful women. We all had children that have now grown up and given us grandchildren. But there is one basic factor we all shared that I think we have passed on—we all had good parents. No, we all had great parents!

I will not take the time or make an effort here to write about my friends' parents. I could do that, but suffice it to say that my friends' parents were good people who worked hard and tried to raise their kids in good homes with the proper expectations and values, a solid education, and the love needed to move on in life. But I will take the time to talk about my parents and the influence they had on me, my life, and, most likely, my children and grandchildren.

Merrill Imel Abell and Russia Edith Willis (yes, I'll admit my parents had unusual names—whoever heard of Imel or Russia?) grew up within just a few miles of each other on farms near Petersburg, Indiana. My mom, known as "Edie" (short for Edith) almost her entire life, was born on August 8, 1914. Her parents, John and Lilly Willis, were farmers who had eleven children, and my mom was the tenth. They certainly were not what you would call "dirt poor," but they were not rich by any means. Dad was born on April 19, 1912, just four days after the *Titanic* sank. He was always known as Merrill. He was one of four children born to Henry and Grace Abell. Dad had an older brother, Paul, and a younger brother and sister, Oral (Jim) and Mildred.

Dad's family was also a farm family but with a slightly different slant. Although my grandfather Henry worked a small farm, he was also a coal miner in the mines of Pike County in southern Indiana. As the boys and Aunt Mildred grew up, my grandpa would work in the mines and run the farm on the side. Actually, it was the boys and Mildred who worked a good share of the farm while Grandpa made good money in the coal mines. Together, I think they made a good living, especially when the Great Depression hit. The nation still needed coal and the farm crops and livestock provided food and extra money. All I know is that Dad and his brothers worked hard and were pretty stout looking from the photos I have seen of those years. I will never forget one photo that I still have. Dad, Paul, Jim, and Mildred were posing in the picture that was taken shortly after Dad and Mom were married. When showing the picture to my son and daughter, I said, "Look at Papa [my kids' name for my dad]; he's 'cut.' He looks like he could play defensive back for the Colts." Obviously Dad was in his mid-to-late-twenties, still possessing a strong, youthful body, powerful shoulders, narrow waist, and solid muscle for a stomach. His years of hard farm work was apparent in his physique.

Merrill Abell and Edith Willis met near Petersburg, Indiana. I don't know the details. I do know Dad graduated from Petersburg High School in 1933. He was twenty years old when he graduated. I think my mom only completed eighth grade. Regardless, they married on December 28, 1935. Again, I am not completely sure of the chronology, but they moved to the Indianapolis area because Dad took a job in industry at Arvin Industries. They bought a small home in Greenwood, just south of Indianapolis. Within a few years, in the late 1930s, Dad took a job at International Harvester Company (modern-day Navistar), which was located on the south side of Indianapolis. They began raising a family and ended up having three sons. I am the youngest. My oldest brother Don, was born on August 18, 1937. My brother Ron was born on September 12, 1942. I was born somewhat later on November 11, 1949. My parents were in their late thirties when I was born. I know I was not "planned," but my parents loved me just the same, which is another testimony to their faith and values because we all know in our modern-day society what oftentimes happens with unwanted pregnancies.

Merrill and Edith Abell (Mom and Dad)—circa 1935.

Remember my earlier point, that my friends and I all had great parents? That is one of the points of this chapter. I am sure there are exceptions to the "everyone had good parents" line of thinking. And we all could name some examples of parents who were not great. Parents who did awful things. Parents who abandoned their children. Parents who abused their children. Parents who did not support their children. Parents who did not love their children. Parents who did not sacrifice for their children. But I really believe, and have no statistics to back it up, that most parents are good parents who try to do what is best for their children and they sacrifice in multiple ways to accomplish those ends.

My parents, and the majority of parents who lived in their generation, did not abandon their children, did not abuse their children, supported their children, loved their children, and definitely sacrificed for their children. I could give hundreds of examples, as could my brothers, of sacrifices our parents made on our behalf. I can honestly say I have very few "bad" memories involving my parents, and those that are bad usually occurred from circumstances where I did the wrong thing, said the wrong thing, or simply was too immature or stubborn to understand the good guidance my parents gave me.

Mom and Dad, from my earliest recollection, worked hard and provided me with everything I needed to be successful in life. The most important things they gave me were love, encouragement, and security. Isn't it odd that I grew up in the 1950s and '60s—periods of American history that were threatening and tumultuous—two decades full of national and internationals crises. Yet my memories were memories of security. I can still recall those elementary and middle school drills—getting under my desk and covering my head. These were drills for protecting students in case of nuclear disaster. In the 1950s it was believed that should an all-out war between the

United States and the Soviet Union occur, with nuclear weapons being used, approximately one-third to one-half of the world's population would be lost in the holocaust. The world was on the brink of nuclear war in October 1962, with the Cuban Missile Crisis. I was in the seventh grade. Our own President Kennedy was assassinated the next year. The Civil Rights movement with all the demonstrations and racial tension was culminating in the early to mid-60s. I was in late elementary and middle school. The Vietnam War was scaling up in the mid-60s. I was just entering high school. Martin Luther King and Bobby Kennedy were assassinated only two months apart in 1968 near the time of my high school graduation. Amid all this cultural chaos, military threats, and political upheaval, I somehow felt secure and optimistic about my future. Amid all the civil unrest and the threat of nuclear annihilation, I was not afraid—I can't remember entertaining any fearful thoughts. Maybe I was too naïve. Perhaps I was too far removed from the real world. After all, Andy, Barney, and Opie seemed normal. Life in Mayberry went on.

**In back: brothers Ron (L) and Don (R);
in front: Mom, me (John), and Dad—circa 1953.**

I wore nice clothes because my dad and mom worked hard for the income they earned. I am sure they, at times, went without things they wanted just so I had presentable clothes to wear to school and church. I ate well not just because of their income but because my mom only worked when I was in school and every night she prepared a good meal for our table. Her years being raised on a farm with ten brothers and sisters made her a more than adequate presence in the kitchen. She and her four sisters were all excellent cooks. I know because I still carry wonderful memories of some of their great meals. Talk about "home cookin'"!

My dad had good carpentry skills. The years on the farm helped him become proficient with a hammer, nails, a saw, and a planer. He was a good craftsman. When I was only three, Dad and a friend of his, a man who was a home builder by trade, built our "new" home. Our three-bedroom, one-bath, single-car-garage home cost my dad less than eight thousand dollars in 1953.

I know Dad and Mom sacrificed many things to afford that new home. While working at International Harvester for thirty-two years, there were at least two occasions when Dad went on strike with the UAW (United Auto Workers). His union "strike" pay was minimal—far less than was needed to pay the bills. One time he was on strike for several weeks, which meant he did not have a regular paycheck coming in each week. He got a job as a carpenter helping build homes. It was hard work, but he was proactive. He found a job, worked hard, and continued supporting the family until he was called back to International when the strike ended.

Mom and Dad were always "there" for me as I grew up. Although my academic performance in school was well above average and I was certainly motivated to learn, I developed a love of sports also. I began playing organized basketball when I was seven. The next year I played baseball. I continued playing basketball and baseball through my high school years. I can honestly say that as best I can remember, my parents never missed any of my basketball games. I ran cross-country and played baseball in high school also, but those contests sometimes occurred immediately after school, so my parents were not able to attend unless the event was on a weekend. From my own experience as a parent, I know the agony of a sore posterior and stiff back from sitting on wooden bleachers because I have been there for my kids. My parents were loyal, supportive, and almost always present when I played ball. When I needed a new baseball glove in high school, my dad took me to the sporting goods store and basically said, "Pick the glove you need." When I needed some extra money to go on a date or just go out with some friends, my parents slipped me a few bucks. Although I had a few small chores at home (keeping my room picked up, emptying the garbage, mowing the lawn in the summers, etc.), they never pressed me with a large to-do list. I think they realized I was busy enough with my studies and athletic practices, so they wanted to allow me enough time to just be a kid. I am so grateful for that.

After high school I was off to Butler University. Although I earned a half-tuition academic scholarship and worked during the summer months at International Harvester (where I made good money), my parents paid the other half of my tuition. At best, I paid for room and board and books. What a gift! To graduate from Butler University with only a few thousand dollars' of student loan debt was huge. I have my parents to thank for that. Do you think they sacrificed anything to make that happen? I cannot tell you what they sacrificed. A nicer home? A newer car? A better vacation? Perhaps one of these. Maybe all. The point is, I know they sacrificed for me. And, to their credit, they sacrificed for my brothers as well. Only my brothers can talk about those sacrifices.

I know my parents sacrificed significantly for me. But the greatest gift they gave to me did not have a monetary value. From my earliest recollection, I can remember my mom and dad taking me to church on Sunday mornings. What did I learn at church? That answer is very simple: biblical principals that give intrinsic value to life itself. God values life, work, truth, humility, sacrifice, love. Of these you can only put a monetary value on work. My parents modeled these godly elements and taught me to respect them, to love God and to love others. No, my parents were not perfect, but in my mind they were saints. And I am certainly not perfect either. Just ask my wife and kids. But my parents were good people because they lived lives that stood for godly principles. They were dedicated, loving, and sacrificial parents, modeling wholesome values, serving as living examples of what is good and godly in people.

My mom was diagnosed with Alzheimer's when she was in her mid-70s. My dad loved my mom. He stayed by her side until the day she died. He did his best, while in his late 70s and into his 80s, to give quality care to my mom while her Alzheimer's progressed. She continually got worse, losing her capacity to care for herself. Dad cooked and cleaned and cleaned up after Mom. I know it was difficult. Finally, after years of the disease taking its toll, with a great deal of hesitation and a lot of unwarranted guilt, my dad realized he could no longer care for her needs. He reluctantly placed her in a nursing home. The facility was about a ten-minute drive from his home. For more than three years he faithfully visited her. If he missed a day it was only because he was sick. It was common for him to visit Mom twice a day. He would visit at lunchtime and at suppertime. Both times he would sit with her and feed her. He was a trooper ... a dedicated, caring, loving husband. What a model! What an example! What an inspiration!

**Standing behind our dad, John (L), Don, and Ron (R)—
Christmas, 2006.**

I married the love of my life, Gloria, on December 31, 1971. I have already told you about her father, Charles Setser, in Chapter 1. He was the World War II POW. I am sure Gloria could tell the same kind of stories about her mom and dad that I told about my parents. And I know my high school "bucket list" friends could tell the same kind of stories about their parents. That is just what good parents do—sacrifice for their children. Good parents love their kids and would sacrifice even life itself for them.

God's love for us is perhaps best exemplified in the love of a parent for his or her child. The essence of that kind of love is sacrifice. It is doing what is best for the child, no matter the cost, even if the price tag is life itself. God's love is unconditional. It is love that is given without strings attached. It is, in essence, a gift.

God's divine, omniscient love for us knows and wants what is best for us. And God, in his infinite wisdom, did everything possible, without taking away man's free will, to redeem us unto himself. We will look deeper into God's unconditional, authentic, demonstrative love in the final chapters.

Last evening my wife and I went to the movies. We are not avid moviegoers, but we wanted to see the new film *Courageous*. The movie is about four police officers, their newfound friend, Javier, and their respective families. Although the movie is well done, one has to remember that the actors are not Hollywood's top names. The acting is mediocre-to-good. But that is not the point. The real issue is the important moral and ethical points the movie makes—something dreadfully lacking in most Hollywood productions today. *Courageous* is actually the fourth movie from Sherwood Pictures, which is the moviemaking ministry of the Sherwood Baptist Church in Albany, Georgia. The movie hits home for anyone who longs for a principled lifestyle that teaches sound moral and ethical concepts that promote human dignity, justice, and love. It is especially impactful for men who desire to be courageous enough to take full responsibility for their families and then to move forward with a bold and clear resolution for their futures based on biblical principles.

The following "resolution" is the commitment the police officers make in *Courageous:*

"I do solemnly resolve before God to take full responsibility for myself, my wife, and my children.

"I will love them, protect them, serve them, and teach them the Word of God as the spiritual leader of my home.

"I will be faithful to my wife, to love and honor her, and be willing to lay down my life for her as Jesus did for me.

"I will bless my children and teach them to love God with all of their hearts, all of their minds, and all of their strength.

"I will train them to honor authority and live responsibly.

"I will confront evil, pursue justice, and love mercy.

"I will pray for others and treat them with kindness, respect, and compassion.

"I will work diligently to provide for the needs of my family.

"I will forgive those who have wronged me and reconcile with those I have wronged.

"I will learn from my mistakes, repent of my sins, and walk with integrity as a man answerable to God.

"I will seek to honor God, be faithful to His Church, obey His Word, and do His will.

"I will courageously work with the strength God provides to fulfill this resolution for the rest of my life and for His Glory.

"As for me and my house, we will serve the Lord" (Joshua 24:15).[1]

Although there were many points that are worth noting about *Courageous*, one of the most important concepts was related to the character Nathan Hayes, played by Ken Bevel. Hayes was a black deputy sheriff who never met his own father. His mother had actually birthed multiple children by three different men. However, Hayes had a "father," a mentor who took Nathan under his wing and guided, taught, and loved him like a son. Although deputy sheriff Nathan Hayes regretted never having developed a relationship with his biological father, there is no question he loved and respected his adopted father with all his heart. The point here is that we can all impact the world for good. We can all find someone to help and mentor. We can all find a single cause, or even multiple causes that exist for the good of others, that we can support or causes where we can become directly involved. There are so many reputable causes in the world today that make a difference—restoring destroyed lives, feeding the hungry, bringing hope to those who have no hope, rescuing those who have been prostituted and sold into human slavery, and the list goes on and on. How did we move from good parents to becoming involved in societal changes that impact the lives of the less fortunate? Because that is what good parents do. Good parents raise their children with a godly conscience. Good parents teach their children to love others. Good parents teach their children to serve others with love and compassion.

However, we must remember that there are millions of children around the world who have not had the blessing of good parents or at least parents who are able to provide for their basic needs. These children, mostly orphaned, fight to survive every day just to live. The World Health Organization estimates that one-third of the world is well-fed, one-third is underfed, and one-third is starving. Every year between ten and twelve million children die of hunger. If you do the math, one child under the age of five dies every three seconds due to preventable illness or malnutrition (starvation). That is thirty thousand every day![2] Tragic! Unconscionable! Unacceptable! Throughout the 1990s more than one hundred million children died from preventable illness and starvation.[3] To say the least, these statistics are shocking and completely unacceptable. There are numerous ways a person can make small or large sacrifices to address the unnecessary and catastrophic starvation of the millions of lives of innocent children.

At this point, please allow me to plant a seed in the reader's mind. Allow me to give you just a few examples of organizations that serve humanity for the purpose of uplifting the human condition, meeting basic human needs, and restoring justice to those who have lived in a quagmire of poverty, oppression, and inhumanity. The list is not in any way an attempt to recruit support or advertise for these organizations. It is simply a short list of organizations that I have become acquainted with whose principles and missions are to restore dignity to the oppressed, and in doing so, these organizations maintain high ethical standards based on godly principles.

- World Vision International—a partnership of Christians around the world dedicated to working for the world's most vulnerable people. WV is a Christian advocacy and development organization that promotes the welfare of oppressed and helpless people by providing the essentials for life—food, clothing, and shelter. (www.worldvision.org)
- Habitat for Humanity International—founded in 1976 with the idea that "what the poor need is not charity but capital, not caseworkers but coworkers." Habitat has built more than five hundred thousand homes worldwide. It does not provide handouts, just a helping hand. Through the work

of Habitat, thousands of low-income families have found new hope in the form of affordable housing. Churches, community groups, and others have joined to successfully tackle a significant social problem—decent housing for all. (www.habitat.org)

- Fellowship of Associates of Medical Evangelism—although officially formed in 1970, FAME's roots go back to the vision of Dr. Dennis Pruett, who foresaw a mission organization that would reach around the world. FAME provides medical supplies, facilities, staff, and programming to render assistance around the world training nationals to become healthcare providers and educators. (www.fameworld.org)

- Life in Abundance International—in east Africa, LIA serves the poorest of the poor regardless of religious or political affiliation. It empowers churches to serve the poor using a holistic approach for community transformation. HIV/AIDS, poverty, and orphaned/vulnerable children devastate the physical, psychological, educational, and emotional fabric of the communities of East Africa. LIA strives tirelessly to meet the needs of the oppressed and deprived in East Africa. (www.liaint.org)

- International Justice Mission—founded in 1997, IJM is an organization with a slightly different slant on helping the oppressed around the world. To this point in time, little had been done to actually restrain the oppressors who are a source of great harm to the vulnerable. Gary Haugen, working as a lawyer at the US Department of Justice and as the United Nations' investigator-in-charge in the aftermath of the Rwandan genocide, founded International Justice Mission as a response to this massive need. Today, more than three hundred professionals work tirelessly to confront aggressive human violence: violence that strips widows and orphans of their property and livelihoods, violence that steals dignity and health from children trafficked into forced prostitution, violence that denies freedom and security to families trapped in slavery. (www.ijm.org)

- Kids against Hunger—a family-friendly program of A Child's Hope International, where people of all ages work to provide lifesaving food for starving children. Kids against Hunger is a widely acclaimed component of A Child's Hope International Humanitarian Relief program, which provides fresh water wells, medical supplies, clothing, and other essentials for the children of the world. (www.kidsagainsthunger.org)

- Horizon International, Inc.—a non-profit Christian relief and development organization whose purpose is to minister to orphaned children who have been affected by HIV/AIDS. HIV/AIDS orphaned children are served regardless of race, gender, or religion with the purpose of breaking the cycle of poverty that so often entraps them and to free them from poverty and disease. (www.horizoninternationalinc.com)

On the weekend of October 8-9, 2011, and again one year later on October 13-14, 2012, a total of more than three thousand people per year from my local church body—Northview Church in Carmel, Indiana—donated ten thousand hours of service to community-related projects. Volunteers engaged in service tasks from cleaning homes and raking leaves for older shut-ins, to painting and cleaning up at community centers and schools, to packaging meals for starving children in Africa (more than eighty thousand meals were packaged for Kids against Hunger). Each year more than sixty groups performed work projects that helped someone else. It is this exact kind of small individual and group sacrifices that we all need to invest and participate in to make our communities, our nation, and our world, a better place. Small sacrifices can bring about large changes.

"The only thing necessary for the triumph of evil is for good men to do nothing." This statement, attributed to Edmund Burke, the renowned British statesman, author, orator, and political analyst, has a simple and direct meaning - evil will creep in if good people stand by and do nothing.

My parents taught me to care about others. More specifically, they taught me to have compassion for those less fortunate. My parents taught me to sacrifice in my pursuit of helping others. Sounds familiar, doesn't it? Sounds like the teachings of Christ. Anytime we give of ourselves and our resources, anytime we give from the heart with the intention to help another human being, we sacrifice. If we give money to help others, we are giving of ourselves because we spent valuable time earning that money. If we volunteer time, time being a valuable commodity to us all, we are giving a valuable gift because time is precious. Choose your own gifts and support your own charities for the sole purpose of helping those who suffer from oppression and misfortune at home and around the world.

Take time to reflect on the sacrifices others have made that have given you a better life. Sacrifices made by parents, family members, teachers, coaches, friends, neighbors, pastors ... the list goes on and on. Finally, knowing how the sacrifices of others have made your life better, ask the most important question of all—"What am I sacrificing to improve the lives of others?"

Chapter 7

Sacrifices in Early Civilizations

Ascribe to the Lord, O families and nations, ascribe
to the Lord glory and strength, ascribe to the Lord
the glory due his name. Bring an offering and come
before him, worship the Lord in the splendor of his
holiness.

—1 Chronicles 16:28-29 (NIV)

Is the concept of sacrifice an integral component of the human experience? Often, when we consider the concept of sacrifice, we think of a different connotation for the word. Instead of considering the more humane types of sacrifice—those actions intended to improve or assist other individuals, groups, or causes—we sometimes think of the sacrificial systems of early cultures that literally sacrificed animals, grains, food, or other objects to various idols or gods. However, the more radical, ritualistic sacrifice of human beings with the intent of gaining favor with culture-specific gods or idols and securing life's blessings in what we would nowadays consider pagan rituals splattered with the sacrificial blood of humans was also quite prevalent in early civilizations. There are a multitude of ancient cultural examples of this type of sacrificial system since the beginning of recorded history. These systems are too numerous to study at length, but for our purpose, we will mention just a few to give us a reference point from which we can consider the concept of sacrifice.

In the Pentateuch, the Old Testament writings of Moses, Genesis 4:2-5 speaks of Cain and Abel bringing sacrifices to the Lord. Cain "worked the soil" and Abel was a shepherd who "kept flocks". Genesis 4:3 says, "In the course of time Cain brought some of the fruits of the ground an offering unto the Lord" (NIV). The following verse states, "And Abel also brought an offering—fat portions from some of the firstborn of his flock" (NIV). Archeological records show that in most early cultures some form of grain or animal sacrifices were common. Actually, the archaeological record contains human and animal corpses with sacrificial marks long before any written records of the practice.[1]

Although the use of food grains as sacrifices were common from early times, the blood sacrifices appear to be more common in ancient cultures. Animal sacrifice is the killing of an animal as part of a religious or cultural ritual system. Blood sacrifices were practiced by adherents of many religions and cultures as a means of appeasing a god or gods or with the intent of changing the course of nature. Blood sacrifice also served a social or economic function in those cultures, where the edible portions of the animal were distributed among those attending the sacrifice for consumption. Animal sacrifice in one form or another has been traced to nearly all cultures. From the ancient Hebrews to the Greeks and Romans (specifically the cleansing ceremony Lustratio), from the early Egyptians (for example in the cult of Apis) and the Aztecs (Central America) to the Incas (South America) and the Yoruba (Africa), blood sacrifices were utilized. Animal sacrifice is still practiced today by the followers of

Santería and other lineages of Orisha as a means of curing the sick and giving thanks to the Orisha (spirits or deities representing the god Olodumare).[2]

History also records many cultures that practiced human sacrifice as well. Without going into the gory details, suffice it to say that in Asia, human sacrifices were made to various gods and goddesses. It has been reported that children were sacrificed in India. Human sacrifice in Europe was mainly performed to protect buildings from weather, war, or the devil. The victims were usually illegitimate children bought from their mother for that purpose. As the Aztecs migrated into central Mexico, their priests modified their gods into fearful, bloodthirsty beings who could only be appeased with human sacrifices. In this religion of conquest, Montezuma and his Aztecs believed the greatest honor a warrior could have was to die in battle or to volunteer as a sacrifice to the gods in a religious ceremony. In South America, the Incas are known to have sacrificed healthy young children upon the Andean peaks to their mountain deities. Several of these mummified victims, some with their skulls bashed in, are on display in modern museums.[3]

Closer to the religious roots of Christianity, the blood sacrifices of animals were a dominant and central feature in the history of the Hebrews of the Old Testament. Jews today do not employ any kind of animal sacrifice in worship ceremonies, nor have Jews offered sacrifices since the destruction of Jerusalem (and the Temple) in the first century. There are some Orthodox Jewish rabbis in Israel who keep the techniques and laws of sacrifice alive by practicing the techniques of ritual sacrifice and teaching young Orthodox boys and men the techniques and laws related to religious sacrifices, but these practices are not used in a public worship venue. The practice of Hebrew ritual sacrifice effectively stopped when the Roman army destroyed the Holy Temple in Jerusalem in 70 AD. There was a brief resumption of sacrifices during the Jewish War of 132-135 AD. However, after this war was lost, sacrificial offerings ended. Since the Holy Temple has been destroyed Jews are unable, due to ceremonial specifications, to employ any sacrificial offerings in modern-day Jewish religious ceremonies. It is believed that when the Messiah returns, the Holy Temple will be rebuilt and sacrifices will once again be utilized.[4]

The following paragraphs are an extremely brief history of the Jewish Temple and worship in Jerusalem. Do not get bogged down in the names and dates. We want to remain on task with the theme of sacrifice, which was a major part of the Temple worship experience. The intent is that the reader gain a general understanding of the approximate one thousand-year history of the two Jewish temples. The Hebrew Bible reports that the First Temple was built in 957 BC by King Solomon, the son of King David, who reigned from about 970-930 BC. The Temple was the only place where Jewish sacrifices could be offered. The Temple replaced the portable sanctuary (tabernacle) constructed in the Sinai Desert when Moses and the children of Israel were wondering in the wilderness of the Sinai after fleeing Egypt. This first Temple was partially destroyed a few decades later by Sheshonk I, Pharaoh of Egypt. Efforts were made at partial reconstruction but it was not until 835 B.C. that Jehoash, King of Judah in the second year of his reign, spent large sums of treasure in a Temple reconstruction effort. More than a hundred years later, the Temple was stripped again by Sennacherib, King of Assyria, sometime about 700 BC. The First Temple was totally destroyed when Jerusalem was overrun by the Babylonians in 586 BC.

Cyrus the Great, according to the book of Ezra, began construction of the Second Temple. This occurred in 538 BC. Babylon had fallen the year before. The Second Temple was completed twenty-three years later in the sixth year of the reign of Darius the Great and was dedicated by the Jewish governor Zerubbabel. The Temple was nearly destroyed again in 332 BC because the Jews would not acknowledge the deification of Alexander the Great of Macedonia. After the death of Alexander in 323 BC, with the Macedonian Empire being dismembered piecemeal, the Ptolemies came to rule over Judea and the Temple. Under the Ptolemies, a Greek dynasty that ruled Egypt, the Jews were given many civil liberties and lived content under their rule. However, when the Ptolemaic army was defeated at Panium by Antiochus III of the Seleucids (a Greek-Macedonian dynasty) in 198 BC, things changed dramatically. Antiochus wanted to bring the Hellenistic culture to the Jews, attempting to introduce the Greek pantheon (all gods of the Greek people) into the temple. A Jewish rebellion ensued but was brutally crushed. When Antiochus died in 187 BC, his son, Seleucus IV Philopator, succeeded him. However, his policies never took effect in Judea because he was assassinated the year after he took control of Judea.

If you get bored quickly with history, please stay with me just a little longer to understand the historical link to Hebrew Temple worship.

Antiochus IV Epiphanes succeeded his older brother to the Seleucid throne. He immediately put into place his father's previous policy of universal Hellenisation. Again the Jews rebelled and Antiochus retaliated in force. The Jews became incensed when the religious observance of the Sabbath and Circumcision were outlawed.

When Antiochus erected a statue of Zeus in the Temple and began sacrificing pigs on the alter, their anger could not be controlled. When a Greek official asked a Jewish priest to perform a pagan sacrifice, the priest (Mattathias), killed him. Antiochus, now nearly in a state of rage, resorted to the same bloody reprisals. In 167 BC, the Jews rose up en masse behind Mattathias to fight and win their freedom from Seleucid tyranny. Judas Maccabeus, the son of Mattathias, rededicated the temple in 165 BC, and the Jews celebrate this event to this day as a major part of the festival of Hanukkah.

Although the Temple had now been rededicated, the time for reinstated Temple worship (and sacrifice) was short-lived. In a little more than one hundred years, the temple was desecrated again in 54 BC by the Roman general and politician Marcus Licinius Crassus. When news of this reached the Jews, they revolted again, only to be put down in 43 BC. The Temple was renovated again around 20 BC by Herod the Great, and it became known as Herod's Temple (the temple where Hebrew worship and sacrifices occurred during the life of Christ). During the Roman occupation of Judea, the Temple remained under control of the Jewish people. It was later destroyed by the Romans in 70 AD during the Roman siege of Jerusalem. The destruction of Jerusalem and the Temple within that city was no small thing. The Jewish historian Josephus wrote that during the Roman army's siege of Jerusalem, more than one million inhabitants of the city were killed. Much of the city was leveled by the Roman army.[5]

So why the summary of the history of the Jewish Temples in Jerusalem? The main point is that the reader understands that for a significant portion of Jewish history—about a thousand years (957 BC-70 AD)—there was, though interrupted at times, a central place of worship and sacrifice in Jerusalem whose history remains even today as an integral component of the Jewish faith. The Western Wall, as it is called today, is the most holy place accessible to the Jewish people because of Muslim control of the Temple Mount. Known in recent centuries as the "Wailing Wall," it was built by Herod the Great as the retaining wall of the Temple Mount complex. The plaza that contains the wall was created as an area for prayer when Israel captured the city of Jerusalem in 1967. In present-day Israel, thousands of people gather at the wall for prayer. Also remember that from the time of the Exodus (the liberation of the Hebrews from slavery in Egypt under Pharaoh that culminated in the presentation of the law tablets—the Ten Commandments—to Moses on Mount Sinai) the "tabernacle" served as the traveling holy place until the conquering of the land of Canaan and its occupation by the nomadic nation of Israelites (no one knows the specific date but probably sometime about 1500-1400 BC). The tabernacle continued to be the worship tent and place of sacrifice until the building of the first Temple in 957 BC.

We are now getting to the really important stuff—the true "nitty-gritty" of the cultural and religious sacrificial system of the Jews. In the most holy inner chamber of the tabernacle (and later the Temple) was a room. This room was divided by a huge, heavy tapestry (veil) on which images of the cherubim (originally angels that God placed in the Garden of Eden after the expulsion of Adam and Eve to guard the way to the Tree of Life) were woven. The area created behind the veil represented what is in heaven. The word "veil" in the Hebrew language means a screen, a divider, or a separator that hides something. What was this woven tapestry hiding? Essentially, it was shielding a Holy God from sinful man. Whoever entered into this most holy place, the Holy of Holies, was entering into the very presence of God. In fact, anyone who entered the Holy of

Holies would die. The only exception was the high priest on the Day of Atonement. Even the high priest, God's chosen mediator with his people, could only pass through the veil and enter this sacred dwelling once a year. Even as the high priest entered, he had to make some meticulous, God-ordained preparations: he had to literally cleanse himself, put on special religious clothing, bring to the Holy of Holies a burning incense so that the smoke would cover his eyes from a direct view of God, and the high priest must bring blood with him to make atonement for sins.

Hebrews 9:7 says, "But only the high priest entered the inner room, and that only once a year, and never without blood, which he offered for himself and for the sins the people had committed in ignorance" (NIV). This room was called the Holy of Holies because it was the holiest place in the tabernacle (or the Temple) where the Ark of the Covenant rested. Yes, this is the same Ark of the Covenant referred to in the classic movie *Raiders of the Lost Ark*. At one point in the movie, Indiana Jones, speaking to his college supervisor, Dr. Marcus Brody, referred to the possible find of the lost ark as "everything we got into archeology for."

On the lid of the Ark of the Covenant, which was called the mercy seat (or atonement cover), was a depiction of the description found in Genesis 3:24: "he placed on the east side of the garden of Eden cherubim and a flaming sword flashing back and forth to guard the way to the tree of life" (NIV). The cherubim (angels), symbols of God's divine presence and power, were facing downward toward the ark with outstretched wings that protruded over the mercy seat. The whole structure was forged and molded out of one piece of pure gold. The atonement cover was God's dwelling place in the tabernacle. It was the earthly representation of God's throne, flanked by angels.[6]

In Leviticus 16:13-16, the high priest goes into the "Holy of Holies" once a year to sprinkle blood on the mercy seat for the sins of the people, "make atonement for the most holy place because of the uncleanness [sin] and rebellion of the Israelites, whatever their sins have been" (NIV). And in Hebrews 9:7, it says, "But only the high priest entered the inner room (Holy of Holies), and that only once a year, and never without blood, which he offered for himself and for the sins the people had committed in ignorance" (NIV).

Remember, the Ark of the Covenant contained the "law of God." The Ark actually contained three things: (1) a gold jar of manna (the bread that God provided to sustain the Israelites in the wilderness of the Sinai); (2) Aaron's staff, which budded, and (3) the stone tablets given by God to Moses upon which were written the Ten Commandments. Obviously the Ark was a sacred and holy vessel ordained by God with a specific purpose. When the high priest applied the blood to the mercy seat (also called the "lid of covering"), it became effective (the active agent) as the blood sacrifice. Thus the "law" (God's law of righteousness represented by the Ten Commandment tablets within the ark) could not testify against the sins of the people. God promised that when he saw the blood, it would "cover over" (lid of covering) the sins of Israel—hence the name "atonement cover." God no longer would see the people's sin, only the blood atonement that would appease his wrath against unrighteousness.[7]

In Exodus 25:22 we find the words, "There, above the cover between the two cherubim that are over the Ark of the Covenant law, I will meet with you and give you all my commands for the Israelites" (NIV).

As mentioned earlier, many ancient cultures and religions utilized some form of animal and even human blood sacrifice. But the use of sacrificial blood in the Hebrew culture, a key element in the Jewish religion, is entirely different. The Hebrews, and the history of civilization itself, validate the person of Moses. Moses was a great and upcoming leader in the house of Pharaoh in Egypt. However, God intervened and chose Moses to become the "great deliverer" of the enslaved Hebrew people. God's active intervention in the life of Moses, Aaron, David, and others are well documented in Old Testament writings as well as other Jewish historical texts. The use of animal blood sacrifices in Jewish worship ceremonies was under specific instruction given by God to Moses, just as the Ten Commandments were delivered unto Moses by God's intervention on Mount Sinai.

One keyword in Jewish temple worship mentioned in our earlier discussion was "atonement." Each October the Jewish community celebrates Yom Kippur, or the Day of Atonement, the holiest day on the Jewish religious calendar. The Jewish (Old Testament) scriptures state that Aaron, Israel's great high priest (Ha-Gadol) was commanded to kill a goat once a year and then sprinkle its blood upon the alter in a sacred area of the Temple called The Holy of Holies (Kiddush Kiddushim). Leviticus 17:11 specifically states, "It is the blood that makes atonement for one's life" (NIV). Nothing else … not fasting, not prayer, not charitable giving, nothing could replace or replicate the sacrificial blood to bring about God's desired end—forgiveness and thence, a restored relationship with God, which had been broken by sin.[8]

We should learn several things from this act of worship and sacrifice. First, Aaron, the first high priest ordained of God, made atonement for the Hebrew people, indicating that the people needed a mediator to represent them before God. Secondly, an innocent victim, in this case a goat or a lamb without blemish, had to be killed for them represented by the sprinkled blood on the mercy seat of God. Third, another goat, actually a "scapegoat," was released and designated to symbolically "take away" their sins. And finally, each Jewish person had to put their faith in this sacrificial act performed by God's high priest, in order to receive atonement.[9] So it was by personal faith based on an act of sacrifice that the Jew could be forgiven. By the way, if you have not yet come to a conclusion on the definition of atonement, it could be defined as "to cover, to wipe out, to cleanse, to appease, and to purge."[10] In Romans 5:11 of the King James Bible, the Greek word that is translated as "atonement" means "reconciliation." Through this act of sacrifice, the Jew would become reconciled to God.

All this was fine for the Hebrews back in biblical times, right? But the question for us, Jew or non-Jew, in the twenty-first century is, "What blood is used today?" If God required a specific blood sacrifice to cleanse the sins of the people, and there are no longer sacrifices being made with blood to be sprinkled on the mercy seat of the Ark of the Covenant, then how can God, according to his own instruction, forgive human sin? We have already made the point that Jewish use of blood sacrifice has not existed in any kind of sustained ceremonial form since around the second century. And, who is the "mediator" (high priest) who reconciles sin-laden man to a righteous and holy God? The answer, at least in modern-day Judaism is that in 70 AD, the Romans destroyed the Temple and Jerusalem. Jewish rabbis decided to restructure Judaism without a blood sacrificial system and thus arbitrarily substituted fasting, prayer, charitable giving, and repentance as the worship elements that would take the place of the blood sacrifice. Still, the real question remains, despite the arbitrary substitution system devised by the first century Jewish rabbis, "Has God terminated sacrificial atonement as the only basis upon which man can receive God's forgiveness?"

The Hebrew prophet Isaiah, writing sometime in the eighth-century BC, foretold that a "suffering servant" would, in a future time, die for the sins of Israel. The prophet wrote in the fifty-third chapter of Isaiah, "he was despised and rejected by mankind ... he took up our pain and bore our suffering ... he was pierced for our transgressions, he was crushed for our iniquities; the punishment that brought us peace was on him and by his wounds we are healed...and the Lord has laid on him the iniquity of us all ... he was led like a lamb to the slaughter ...yet it was the Lord's will to crush him and cause him to suffer...the Lord makes his life an offering for sin... because he poured out his life unto death, and was numbered with the transgressors...he bore the sin of many, and made intercession for the transgressors" (NIV).

These all point to the death of a Messiah, the Christ. A humble son of a carpenter, who began his ministry as a Jewish rabbi near the age of thirty about two thousand years ago, claimed to be that "suffering servant." He claimed divinity and that He was the Messiah of Israel. He lived a sinless life and performed amazing miracles of healing as well as miracles demonstrating his power over physical things (turning water to wine, walking on water, creating enough food to feed five thousand from a few fish and loaves of bread, and many other miracles), and ultimately of physical healing and raising the dead to life. After a horrible crucifixion and entombment for three days, He revealed himself to hundreds, showing his nail-scarred hands and spear-pierced side. Jesus Christ fulfilled hundreds of Old Testament prophecies by becoming the atoning sacrifice foreshadowed in the blood sacrifices of the Tabernacle and the Temple. He died for the sins of the world. His name was Yeshua HaMashiach, Jesus the Messiah.[11]

The concept of sacrifice is as old as man himself. Nearly every civilization in recorded history appears to have some system or reference to a form or forms of sacrifice. However, none compare or have the underlying spiritual truth found in the God-ordained and inspired sacrificial system of the Hebrews. It is only in the nomenclature and symbolism of the Hebrew tabernacle and Temple system of sacrifice (which God gave to Moses and that he wrote meticulously about in the Old Testament books of Exodus and Leviticus) that we can begin to understand what the Old Testament Scriptures and prophecies were pointing to … to ultimately and finally cleanse the unrighteous nature of man, God himself provided an unmerited gift, a sacrifice … Yeshua HaMashiach.

Chapter 8

The Ultimate Sacrifice

But they shouted, "Take him away! Take him away!
Crucify him." "Shall I crucify your king?" Pilate
asked. "We have no king but Caesar," the chief priests
answered. Finally Pilate handed him over to them
to be crucified. So the soldiers took charge of Jesus.
Carrying his own cross, he went out to the place of
the Skull (which in Aramaic is called Golgotha). Here
they crucified him, and with him two others—one on
each side and Jesus in the middle.

—John 19:15-18 (NIV)

It sounds so simple, doesn't it? It is like saying Pearl Harbor was
bombed by the Japanese on December 7, 1941. Or terrorists flew
planes into the Twin Towers in New York City and the Pentagon in
Washington, DC on September 11, 2001. The statements make it
sound too simple, as if no one suffered, no one died, no one sacrificed.
We all know Pearl Harbor and 9/11 were not that simple. The horror,
bloodshed, and tragedy linked to these two singular American
historical events cannot be communicated with mere words. Those
awful two days in America's history were unspeakably disastrous, and
the repercussions have impacted America in countless ways.

Christ's death on Calvary was not that simple either. Actually, it was quite complicated, and the impact of that singular event on the life of every human being is not only critical, it is eternal. Jesus' death on Golgotha was the end of his suffering. What we often do not consider is that his death was preceded by events that were shocking, terrible, and filled with more suffering and pain than we realize and often conveniently forget. What we should also remember is that Jesus knew his destiny. One completely unique and, quite honestly, horrible characteristic of Christ's human existence on earth was that he knew what the future held. He knew his mission. He knew the sacrifice and suffering that was before him. He willingly went to Jerusalem to fall into the trap set for him by the chief priests and Pharisees. He willingly surrendered himself to the authorities. He willingly went to the cross. He willingly sacrificed himself. He was the innocent, spotless Lamb of God, slain for the sins of the world foretold in more than three hundred prophecies found in Old Testament Scripture.

Jesus was arrested by Roman soldiers accompanied by some Jewish officers. He was given six illegal trials before various magistrates, each trying to "pawn off" Jesus onto another to avoid controversy. He was finally convicted and condemned to suffer a punishment that was usually reserved for the Roman Empire's worst criminals. The arrest of Jesus was the result of the betrayal of Judas, one of his disciples. Jesus was betrayed for money—thirty pieces of silver. His trials were a judicial farce and his convictions were illegal according to both Roman and Jewish law. Therefore, it goes unsaid that his sentencing and punishment was a complete travesty of justice.

The arrest of Jesus in the garden of Gethsemane on the Mount of Olives set in motion a series of six trials—three before the Jewish religious authorities and three before the Roman civil authorities. A

Hebrew document called the *Mishnah*, authored around 200 AD, recorded the oral religious and legal traditions established by the Jewish people over centuries. A portion of the *Mishnah* presents the guidelines governing the Sanhedrin, the ruling council responsible for conduct of trials and hearings and rendering of religious and civil decisions. According to the *Mishnah*, "no trials were to occur during night hours before the morning sacrifice."[1] Also, all trials were to be public. Secret trials were forbidden. Trials were to be held in the Hall of Judgment of the Temple. Capital cases required a minimum of twenty-three judges. An accused person could not testify against himself. Someone (representative counsel) was required to speak on behalf of the accused. Conviction required the testimony of two or three witnesses. Witnesses for the prosecution were to be cross-examined extensively. Capital cases were to follow a strict order or argumentation—for defense and prosecution. The high priest could not participate in the questioning. Each witness in a capital case was to be examined individually, not in the presence of other witnesses. The testimony of two witnesses found to be in contradiction rendered both invalid. Verdicts in capital cases were to be handed down in daylight hours. Members of the Sanhedrin were to meet in pairs all night, discuss the case, and reconvene for the purpose of confirming the final verdict. All of these guidelines from Jewish law were violated in the Jewish trials of Jesus, which included his trial before Annas, Caiaphas, and finally before the Sanhedrin.[2]

The first trial of Jesus is recorded in the gospel of John 18:12-23. Scripture indicates that after Jesus was seized at Gethsemane, He was taken to Annas. Annas had been high priest but was removed by Valerius Gratus in AD 15. His son-in-law, Caiaphas, became high priest, but many argued that Annas was still the power behind the office. In this so-called "trial," at least a half-dozen points of order were ignored: the trial took place at night, during the week of Passover, in secret, and not in the Temple's Hall of Judgment, to name a few. If Annas was playing the role of high priest (which technically he was not), he was not allowed by Jewish law to participate in the questioning and was not to ask Jesus to testify against himself, which he did. Even Jesus pointed to the fact that witnesses should have been easy to find but none were present.[3]

In the second trial of Jesus, the Lord was brought before the "real" high priest of the Sanhedrin. Caiaphas, again in the same manner of "illegalism" as high priest should not have been part of the questioning. Regardless, when Caiaphas said to Jesus, "I charge you under oath by the living God: tell us if you are the Christ, the Son of God" (Matthew 26:63, NIV). "Yes, it is as you say," Jesus replied. "But I say to all of you: In the future you will see the Son of Man sitting at the right hand of the Mighty One and coming on the clouds of heaven" (Matthew 26:64, NIV).

When Jesus claimed to be the Messiah, Caiaphas tore his clothes and declared, "He has spoken blasphemy!" (Matthew 26:65, NIV).

On the surface, one might be impressed with what appears to be the notable religious zeal of Caiaphas. But the zeal of Caiaphas had nothing to do with religion. Both Caiaphas and Annas wanted Jesus dead for two specific reasons. First, Jesus had defied the authority of the high priest's control over the Temple. As you may recall, Jesus had vehemently thrown the "moneychangers" out of the Temple ... loss of revenue for someone! Secondly, and more importantly, Jesus was bad for "religious" business. Directly or indirectly, Jesus was challenging the power of the high priest and his associates in the Temple. Annas (and Caiaphas) and their family held a monopoly on the animals sacrificed in the Temple. The temple priests determined which animals were acceptable for sacrifice. And, Annas (and Caiaphas) controlled the priests. Jesus had made a spectacle in the temple by forcing out the moneychangers and declaring the commercialization of the Temple an affront to God. Jesus and his followers were questioning and confronting the monetary implications of the temple "tax" tics (political and monetary tactics of the Temple), which were under the control, and in secret lining the pockets, of Caiaphas and his family.[4] Is it not interesting that both reasons were related to power and money?

In the third Jewish trial, Jesus was brought before the Sanhedrin, the ruling Jewish council (in essence, the Jewish Supreme Court). This trial is recorded in Matthew 27, Mark 15 and Luke 22. Remember that the Sanhedrin had no authority under Roman rule to put anyone to death. The point of emphasis for the Sanhedrin was the claim of Jesus that he was the Messiah. Their strategy was to convince the Roman authorities to kill Jesus, thinking that Rome would want to rid Judea of a potential revolutionary, inflammatory and potentially dangerous figure. After all, in the minds of the Romans, this popular Jesus could lead an uprising of the Jews. Also, in the minds of the Jewish religious leaders, if Jesus was executed by the Roman authorities, the Jewish people would then reject him as just another false messiah.[5]

The Sanhedrin next took Jesus to Pilate, the Roman governor assigned to rule over the province of Judea. This was the first of the civil trials. Initially determining that Jesus was under Herod's jurisdiction, Pilate sent Jesus to Herod who was in Jerusalem at the time because he was a Galilean observing the Passover. Herod Antipas was the ruler of Galilee and Perea. But Herod, also not wanting to get involved in this political and religious conflict, sent Jesus back to Pilate. Pilate obviously did not want to get drawn into a religious question and it appears from Scripture that he did not want to take any responsibility for the judgment of Jesus. Finally, when the crowd became unruly and the Jewish leaders reminded him that Jesus' claim to be king was a challenge to Roman rule and to the Roman deification of Caesar, Pilate reluctantly agreed to condemn Jesus to crucifixion only after the Jewish leaders explained to him that Jesus presented a threat to Roman occupation through his claim to the throne of David as king of Israel in the royal line of David.

After releasing Barabbas upon the demand of the people according to a custom of releasing a prisoner at Passover (see Leviticus 16:6-10), Pilate ordered Jesus to be scourged. The scourging scene in Mel Gibson's *The Passion of the Christ* is not a glorified, Hollywood version of what happened to Jesus just for the sake of creating a gory scene for bloodthirsty moviegoers. The scene from the movie gives us a realistic, abhorrent, and sadistic portrayal of what literally happened to people who were scourged under Roman rule. Roman soldiers who were given the scourging detail were trained for this type of torture. I believe there was a sadistic side to the nature of those who carried out this gruesome task. With a brutality much like many of the Nazi SS death squads and concentration camp commandants in World War II, the Roman soldiers who were given the task of scourging prisoners actually enjoyed what they did. They liked inflicting pain and torture. There is no question that Jesus was severely beaten. Jewish law limited the scourging to thirty-nine lashes. The pain and loss of blood, with utmost certainty, would leave the victim in a state of shock. This may account for the inability of Jesus to successfully carry the cross to Golgotha for his crucifixion. Simon of Cyrene was compelled to carry the cross of Jesus because Jesus was too weak after the scourging (Matthew 27:32). On the way to be crucified, the Roman soldiers led Jesus to the common hall where "They stripped him and put a scarlet robe on him, and then twisted together a crown of thorns, and set it on his head. They put a staff in his right hand. Then they knelt in front of him and mocked him. 'Hail, king of the Jews!' they said. They spit on him and took the staff and struck him on the head again and again" (Matthew 27:28-31, NIV). From the beating, Jesus walked on a path now known to us as the "via dolorosa," or the "way of suffering," to be crucified.

Crucifixion was a practice that originated with the Persians and was later passed on to the Carthaginians and the Phoenicians. It was a horrible form of execution. The Romans perfected it as a method of execution that caused maximum pain and suffering over a period of hours. Those crucified included slaves and provincials who were convicted of crimes, as well as the lowest types of criminals. Roman citizens, except perhaps for soldiers who deserted, were not subjected to this barbaric and painful punishment.

The procedure of crucifixion may be summarized as follows. The patibulum (cross beam) was put on the ground and the victim lay upon it. Nails, about seven inches long and with a diameter of roughly 3/8 of an inch were driven into the wrists. The points would go into the vicinity of the median nerve, causing shocks of pain to radiate through the arms. It was possible to place the nails between the bones so no fractures (or broken bones) occurred. Studies have shown that nails were probably driven through the small bones of the wrist, since nails in the palms of the hand would not support the weight of a body. In ancient terminology, the wrist was considered part of the hand. Standing at the crucifixion sites would be upright posts, called stipes, standing about seven feet high. In the center of the stipes was a crude seat called a sedile or sedulum, which served as a support for the victim. The patibulum was then lifted onto the stipe. The feet were then nailed to the stipe. To allow for this, the knees had to be bent and rotated laterally, being left in a very uncomfortable position. The titulus (an inscription or name) was hung above the victim's head.[6] When the cross was erected upright, there was tremendous strain put on the wrists, arms, and shoulders, resulting in a dislocation of the shoulder and elbow joints. The arms, being held up and outward, held the rib cage in a fixed end inspiratory position, which made it extremely difficult to exhale and impossible to take a full breath. The victim would only be able to take very shallow breaths. This may explain why Jesus made very short statements while on the cross. As time passed, the muscles, from the loss of blood, lack of oxygen, and the fixed position of the body, would undergo severe cramping and spasmodic contractions.[7]

Without a doubt, the crucifixion of Jesus occurred. Jesus died on the cross. Roman authority made sure of that. There was no deception. The Roman soldiers were well trained in killing, and the procedures implemented on those who hung on the Roman crosses ensured that no one came off the cross alive. The soldiers given the responsibility of executing criminals could give no excuses explaining why a criminal did not die under sentence of Roman law. They made sure the criminal was dead. Without a doubt Jesus was dead.

But, thank God, that was not the end of the story. Jesus was who he claimed to be—the Son of God, the Messiah, and Savior of man. He lived a life full of miracles, documented in religious and non-religious writings as well. In his book *The Case for Christ*, Lee Strobel writes, "The situation with Jesus is unique—and quite impressive in terms of how much we can learn about him aside from the New Testament."[8]

Assume for a moment the New Testament writings did not exist. "Even without them, what would we be able to conclude about Jesus from ancient non-Christian sources such as Josephus, the Talmud, Tacitus, Pliny the Younger, and others?" According to Edwin Yamauchi, Miami University professor and one of the country's leading authorities on ancient history, "We would still have a considerable amount of important historical evidence; in fact, it would provide a kind of outline for the life of Jesus."[9]

According to Yamauchi, "We would know that first, Jesus was a Jewish teacher; second, many people believed that he performed healings and exorcisms; third, some people believed he was the Messiah; fourth, he was rejected by the Jewish leaders; fifth, he was crucified under Pontius Pilate in the reign of Tiberius; sixth, despite this shameful death, his followers, who believed he was still alive, spread beyond Palestine so there were multitudes of them in Rome by AD 64; and seventh, all kinds of people from the cities and the countryside—men and women, slave and free—worshiped him as God."[10]

This is not only an enormous and impressive amount of independent corroboration, but it gives verification to the fact that Jesus' life can be reconstructed outside the contours of religious literature. And, there is even more that can be gleaned about the life of Jesus from material so old that it actually predates the gospel accounts themselves.[11]

But one amazing piece of evidence still exists regarding the resurrection of Jesus after his crucifixion. Strobel says, "I was reminded of the assessment by one of the towering legal intellects of all time, the Cambridge-educated Sir Norman Anderson, who lectured at Princeton University, was offered a professorship for life at Harvard University, and served as dean of the Faculty of Laws at the University of London. Anderson's conclusion, after a lifetime of analyzing this issue from a legal perspective, was summed up in one sentence: 'The empty tomb, then, forms a veritable rock on which all rationalistic theories of the resurrection dash themselves in vain.'"[12]

Remember our study of the tabernacle and temple sacrifices in the previous chapter? All the high priest's cleansing behaviors that preceded his entry into the Holy of Holies were necessary to present himself and the people of Israel to a righteous God who could not tolerate nor look upon sin. Remember, Habakkuk 1:13 tells us that God's eyes are so pure that he cannot look upon sin. The "mercy seat" with the blood applied was where the blood would change his "judgment seat" of sinful man into a "throne of mercy," literally the "mercy seat" of a forgiving God. Because of the sacrifice of blood offered on that mercy seat, God could not see the sin of the people, only the blood of the sacrifice, and allowed him to offer his mercy through his divine forgiveness.

All the trappings of the "tabernacle" are a symbolic foreshadowing of what Jesus Christ is and what he does for us. Jesus Christ is our Great High Priest (Hebrews 4:14) "who performs all things for us" (Psalm 57:2). Jesus Christ is our sacrifice—the Lamb of God sacrificed for our sin (1 Corinthians 5:7). Jesus Christ is our "mercy seat." He literally covers all our sin with his pure, spotless, holy, sinless blood. Paul, in his letter to the Romans (3:25) uses the Greek word *hilasterion*, which the King James Version translates as "propitiation." The word means atoning sacrifice, atonement cover, or the place where sins are forgiven. In 1 John 2:2 and 4:10, John uses the Greek word *hilasmos*, which the KJV translates also as "propitiation." The word means atoning sacrifice, or the means of forgiveness. In both cases, it is applied directly to Jesus Christ. And so, Jesus Christ, having fulfilled the law with a perfect, sinless life is our "mercy seat." Jesus Christ is our atoning sacrifice. The sacrificial blood of Jesus literally covers our sin so the righteous law of God cannot accuse us. Where there is no law, there is no sin. In the New Testament book of Romans, the apostle Paul, a Pharisee, and a "Hebrew of Hebrews," having full knowledge of the law, declared, "To be sure, sin was in the world before the law was given, but sin is not charged against anyone's account where there is no law" (Romans 5:13, NIV). The shed blood of Jesus Christ changes the "judgment seat" of God into a "throne of mercy"; literally, the "mercy seat" of a loving and forgiving God.[13] The innocent blood of Christ was the atoning sacrifice required by God to satisfy His righteous judgment against sin. A price had to be paid. Jesus paid the required price. No one else could pay the price. No one except Jesus was sinless. Jesus' sinless blood was the price.

So the presence of a Holy God remained shielded from man behind a thick curtain in the Holy of Holies during the history of Israel. However, Jesus' sacrificial death on the cross changed all that. When Jesus died on the cross the curtain in the Jerusalem Temple was torn in half from the top to the bottom (Mark 15:38). Only God could have carried out such an incredible feat because the veil was too high for human hands to have reached it, and too thick to have torn it. The "Holy of Holies" of the Jerusalem temple, a replica of the wilderness tabernacle's holy place, had a curtain (veil) that was about sixty feet in height, thirty feet in width, and four inches thick.

Furthermore, it was torn from top down, meaning this act must have come from above.[14]

There is one instance in time that is a mystery only God knows and understands completely. Remember, as Jesus hung on the cross, he uttered the words, *"Eloi, Eloi, lama sabachthani?"* which means, "My God, my God, why hast Thou forsaken me?" (Matthew 27:16, NIV). I do not believe God had actually forsaken Jesus, but he certainly turned his face away from him. The perfect Father and Son relationship that had existed for eternity changed for a moment. God was unable to look upon his Son because Jesus had become "sin."

In 2 Corinthians 5:21, Paul writes, "God made him who had no sin to be sin for us, so that in him we might become the righteousness of God" (NIV). It is interesting that scholarly research indicates that the verse can and should be translated, "God made him to be 'a sin offering' for us so that we might become God's righteousness." Unbelievable! It is a truly amazing and profound concept—one that only God Himself could conceive. Jesus took all the evil, hateful, and sinful actions of mankind upon himself to make us acceptable in the sight of God. The weight of man's sin must have been the worst pain imaginable ... but not as bad as God turning away from Jesus. In God the Father's holy righteousness, he could not look upon sin—he could not look upon Jesus. His perfect relationship with his Son had been broken ... momentarily. Jesus felt abandoned by God, who had turned his face from him.

However, Jesus did not lose faith in his Father. "Jesus called out with a loud voice, 'Father, into your hands I commit my spirit.' When he had said this, he breathed his last" (Luke 23:46, NIV)).

At the moment Jesus died, the Temple veil was torn and the Holy of Holies was exposed. God's presence was now accessible to all. Shocking as this may have been to the priests ministering in the temple that day, it is indeed good news to us as believers, because we know Jesus' death has atoned for our sins and made us "righteous" before God. The torn veil illustrated Jesus' body, broken for us, thus opening the way for us to come to God. As Jesus cried out "It is finished!" on the cross, He was indeed proclaiming that God's redemptive plan was now complete. The age of animal sacrifices was over. The ultimate sacrifice, Christ (the Messiah) had been presented to and accepted by God. Payment for all our sins had been made. Just like the freedoms we enjoy today as American citizens have been bought at an extreme price—the blood and sacrifice of those soldiers, citizens, and patriots of our nation's history—so our eternal freedom was bought with an even greater price—the blood of Jesus Christ, the Son of God.

We can now boldly enter into God's presence, "We have this hope as an anchor for the soul, firm and secure. It enters the inner sanctuary behind the curtain, where Jesus, who went before us, has entered on our behalf. He has become a high priest forever..." (Hebrews 6:19-20, NIV). "Therefore, brothers, since we have confidence to enter the Most Holy Place by the blood of Jesus, by a new and living way opened for us through the curtain, that is, his body ... let us draw near to God with a sincere heart in full assurance of faith" (Hebrews 10:19-22, NIV). The Holy of Holies is a representation of heaven itself, God's dwelling place, to which we have access now through Christ. In Revelation, John's vision of heaven—the New Jerusalem—also was a perfect square, just as the Holy of Holies was a perfect square (Revelation 21:16). "For Christ did not enter a manmade sanctuary that was only a copy of the true one; he entered heaven itself, now to appear for us in God's presence. Nor did he enter heaven to offer himself again and again, the way the high priest enters the

Most Holy Place every year with blood that is not his own. ... But now he has appeared once for all at the end of the ages to do away with sin by the sacrifice of himself" (Hebrews 9:24-26, NIV).

The bottom line? Let's not lose sight of our original theme—sacrifice. Did Jesus sacrifice? Most certainly. That was God's plan. In the gospel of Mark, Jesus said, "For even the Son of Man did not come to be served, but to serve, and to give his life as a ransom for many" (Mark 10:45, NIV). Consider this: "In your relationships with one another, have the same mindset as Christ Jesus: who, being in very nature God, did not consider equality with God something to be used to his own advantage; rather, he made himself nothing by taking the very nature of a servant, being made in human likeness" (Philippians 2:5-7, NIV)). Jesus, God himself, creator of all things, loved us so much that he *sacrificed* being God and using that status to his advantage to become like us (human) to serve us by meeting our greatest need—redemption. God's story of the redemption of man throughout the Bible is a story of sacrifice. Sacrifice is all about giving. Giving without considering status or position or power. "For God so loved the world (mankind) that he gave his one and only Son, that whosoever believes in him shall not perish but have eternal life" (John 3:16, NIV). God sacrificed. God gave. *For God so loved ...*

But like Sir Arthur Anderson stated, "The empty tomb, then, forms a veritable rock on which all rationalistic theories of the resurrection dash themselves in vain." Had Jesus not been raised from the dead, he not only would have been a notable teacher and prophet, but also he would have been just another Jew who died at the hands of the Roman authorities on a cruel wooden cross. But Jesus, the Messiah, the Anointed One and only Son of God the Father in heaven, was raised from the dead by the Spirit of God on the third day just as prophecies had foretold and just as Jesus said he would.

As far as my research can determine, Christianity is the only world religion where an almighty God sacrifices himself to save his people from destruction. It is also the only religion where a savior who was both human and divine walked the earth, loved his enemies, taught only to love one another, healed the sick, performed a multitude of miracles including raising the dead, and ultimately, was himself raised from the dead, appearing to as many as five hundred at one time after having been pronounced dead.

Chris Tomlin, contemporary Christian artist and musician, composed the song "Jesus Messiah." The lyrics remind us of exactly what I have been writing about.

> "He became sin who knew no sin
> That we might become His righteousness
> He humbled Himself and carried the cross
> Love so amazing ..."[15]

The old hymn "I'd Rather Have Jesus" also has great lyrics that every Christian should take to heart because the lyrics bring us right back to the heart of the gospel. The words are as simple as is the message. Worldly possessions are valueless. Fame is fleeting. The kingdom of Christ is not of this world. Jesus went to the cross to shed his innocent blood as an atoning sacrifice for our sins so that we might have eternal life with God in His kingdom in heaven. Consider the lyrics.

> "I'd rather have Jesus than silver or gold,
> I'd rather be His than have riches untold;
> I'd rather have Jesus than anything
> This world affords today."[16]

The song is simply declaring that the world can give almost anything that mortal man desires. "What good is it for a man to gain the whole world, yet forfeit his soul?" (Mark 8:36, NIV). However, the world and all its treasure cannot give the only gift that has any value—the gift of eternal life. Only Jesus can give that gift. Jesus paid for that gift. He paid for it with the sacrifice of his blood. Jesus—the only name under heaven by which man can be saved. Jesus lived a life verified by recorded history. He literally proved his claim to be the Messiah through the miracles he performed and the prophecies he fulfilled and the greatest proof of all—His resurrection! I am sure there were many miraculous acts that were never recorded because John, the only apostle who did not die a martyr's death, said, "Jesus performed many other signs in the presence of his disciples, which are not recorded in this book. But these are written that you may believe that Jesus is the Messiah, the Son of God, and that by believing you may have life in his name" (John 20:30-31, NIV).

Ultimately, everyone must confront the Christ of history. There is no doubt Jesus lived. There is no doubt Jesus died. There is no doubt Jesus was raised from the dead by the Holy Spirit of God. But the true question of faith that history does record for us, is, "Was Jesus who he said he was?" Was he truly the Son of God? That is a question everyone must answer, and I believe everyone will give an account for that answer when Christ returns (Romans 14:11). I was not at Calvary to witness the cataclysmic events of that day. We do know the earth quaked. The sky grew dark for three hours at midday. The veil of the temple was torn from top to bottom. The earth shook and rocks split. Tombs broke open and many believers who had died were raised from the dead. They came out of their tombs and went into Jerusalem and appeared to many people. But it is recorded that even unbelievers—the Roman centurion and those with him at Calvary, all proclaimed the deity of Jesus. Matthew 27: 54 states, "When the centurion and those with him who were guarding Jesus saw the earthquake and all that had happened, they were terrified, and exclaimed, 'Surely he was the Son of God'" (NIV).

Condense all this to its simplest terms: in the exact same manner of the Hebrew people, *who by faith* believed that at God's direction the high priest's application of blood on the Ark of the Covenant's mercy seat in the Holy of Holies brought justification and forgiveness for their sins, so today, the only hope for a sinful world is *by faith* through God's grace that our forgiveness is possible only through the blood of Jesus Christ in his willful act of sacrifice on the cross at Calvary more than two thousand years ago. And for those who believe in the sin cleansing power of Jesus the Messiah, the inspired Word of God tells us in 1 Peter 2:9, "But you are a chosen people, a royal priesthood, a holy nation, a people belonging to God, that you may declare the praises of him who called you out of darkness [sin] into his wonderful light [the truth of the gospel of Jesus Christ]" (NIV).

Conclusion

As Christ hung on the cross, he said, "Father, forgive them, for they know not what they do." Forgiveness can be, in certain circumstances, a part of sacrifice.

One story of forgiveness that moves my heart is of Kim Phuc. Her photo appeared in newspapers and magazines in the United States and throughout the world on and after June 9, 1972. I had just graduated from Butler University. The week after my graduation, I can still remember seeing Kim's photo the day it appeared in local and national news publications. The photo was so shocking and disturbing … I remember it to this day. The Vietnam War was growing cumbersome as well as psychologically burdensome in America. After years of what seemed to be a never-ending and senseless war that claimed the lives of nearly sixty thousand Americans, that singular piece of photo journalism taken on June 8, 1972, seemed to be the "straw that broke the camel's back." Perhaps the most memorable photograph of the Vietnam War, and certainly the photo that cut to the core of the American conscience, was the picture of Kim Phuc. The picture was one of a nine-year-old Vietnamese girl (Kim) running naked down a roadway, screaming and crying in agony due to napalm (burning jellied gasoline) that clung to her back. The napalm was burning through her skin. Kim's village had been hit by an air napalm attack.[1]

Associated Press photographer Nick Ut earned a Pulitzer Prize for his photograph of the attack's aftermath that day. The photo was also chosen as the World Press Photo of the Year for 1972. The image of Kim Phuc running naked amid the inhumane chaos of war became one of the most haunting images of the Vietnam War.[2]

In his book *How Now Shall We Live?*, Chuck Colson said when he first saw the photo as he climbed into his limousine heading to the White House, "Instinctively, my horrified mind wanted to help this child. I thought involuntarily of my own precious daughter Emily. *What if she had been hurt like this?* Worse, I couldn't avoid a sinking sense of my own responsibility for this young girl's suffering. Her silent scream made me wince. My own skin burned with guilt and shame." Kim's photo impacted people all across America, even Chuck Colson, the hardened political analyst and special counsel to President Richard Nixon.

Interestingly, and thankfully, Kim's story does not end tragically in Vietnam. Soon after the day she was burned, Kim was transported to a hospital in Saigon. A little more than a year later, after seventeen surgeries, Kim was released and sent home. For several years she lived in anonymity, wearing clothing to hide her horrible scars. Kim wanted to be a medical student. The North Vietnamese communist government made many attempts to use her as a propaganda tool extolling the inhumanity and cruelty of American imperialism, even to the point of blackmailing her with the threat of expunging her academic records if she did not cooperate. The government, to keep her "under its thumb," took away all her family's possessions—their home, business, everything but their lives. Being used as a political tool of the government, she became extremely depressed. Kim was given a job in a local library where she read continuously. It was in this library that she read the New Testament for the first time. She eventually attended her sister's church and, in time, accepted Jesus Christ as her Savior.[3]

Kim was allowed to resume her medical studies in 1986. The North Vietnamese government allowed her to go to Cuba to complete her schooling. She met a fellow medical student named Toan. They dated for five years and finally married in 1991. They honeymooned in Moscow and on their return trip to Cuba, their jet aircraft was scheduled to refuel at Gander International Airport in Newfoundland. Kim and Toan decided to take a big risk—to seek political asylum in Canada. Kim told her husband, "If they catch us, they'll send us back to Vietnam, and you know what happens then. They'll kill us."[4]

Believe it or not, she and Toan walked right into the immigration office and told them that they wanted to stay in Canada. With all their clothes still on the plane heading to Cuba, and with only the clothes on their backs, Kim and Toan settled into a thriving Vietnamese community in Toronto. But that's still not the end of the story.

In 1996, Kim Phuc was asked to speak at a Veteran's Day ceremony in Washington, DC. She sat on the platform facing a large crowd of dignitaries and former American veterans—many from the Vietnam War. For Kim, the sight of the sea of uniforms brought back horrible memories of the war.

After some brief comments about who she was and how the war affected her, she made these concluding remarks: "I have suffered a lot from both physical and emotional pain. Sometimes I thought I could not live, but God saved my life and gave me faith and hope." And then she uttered healing words of grace and forgiveness: "Even if I could talk face to face with the pilot who dropped the bomb, I could tell him we cannot change history, but we should try to do good things for the present and for the future to promote peace."

One man, overcome with emotion, rushed to a patrolman and scribbled out a note, asking him to deliver it to Kim. "I'm the man you are looking for," the note read.

When the reporters cleared, Kim turned and looked straight into the man's eyes and then held out her arms ... the same arms she had held out as she ran along the North Vietnamese road in agony from her burning skin. She hugged the man and he began to sob. "I am sorry. I am just so sorry!" he said. "It is okay. I forgive. I forgive," said Kim, echoing her favorite Bible verse, "Forgive, and you will be forgiven"(Luke 6:37, NIV).[5]

By the way, Kim Phuc means "Golden Happiness." What a story of tragedy, struggle, love and forgiveness! For historical purposes, a note of clarification needs to be made at this juncture. The man who sent the note that said, "I'm the man you are looking for" was an American Vietnam veteran, and he was serving in the vicinity of Kim's tragedy when it occurred, but he was not the man who dropped the napalm. That napalm bombing was actually done by a South Vietnamese pilot. I mention this to maintain historical accuracy because a legend has developed that the man at the rally was the pilot. Perhaps he was just a veteran who had his own ghosts to deal with, or he simply felt the need to apologize to Kim. Research indicates he thought he was partially responsible for coordinating the air strike that resulted in Kim's injuries. Regardless, that is not the point of the story. The point is Kim's ordeal, her struggle, and her ability, through God's love, to find forgiveness where bitterness, anger, and hatred could have prevailed. I am sure Kim would give God the credit and the glory for her willingness to forgive.

One hundred forty-eight years ago, our most beloved president gave what is without question the most quoted and remembered speech in the history of the United States. In part, Abraham Lincoln said that November day in 1863, "Four score and seven years ago our fathers brought forth on this continent a new nation, conceived in Liberty ... we are engaged in a great civil war, testing whether that nation, or any nation, so conceived and so dedicated, can long endure ... But in a larger sense, we can not dedicate—we can not consecrate—we can not hallow this ground. The brave men, living and dead, who struggled here, have consecrated it, far above our poor power to add or detract. ... but it (the world) can never forget what they did here. It is for us the living, rather, to be dedicated to the great task remaining before us—that from these honored dead we take increased devotion—that we here highly resolve that these dead shall not have died in vain—that this nation, under God, shall have a new birth of freedom—and that government of the people, by the people, for the people, shall not perish from the earth."

President Lincoln's brief address on November 19, 1863, at the dedication of the national cemetery at Gettysburg, Pennsylvania, is a model of clear, subtle, Lincolnian prose, which gave meaning to the seemingly senseless carnage of war. President Lincoln gave this address, which, by the way, he was still editing on the train to Gettysburg, with the direct intent of honoring those who had valiantly sacrificed their lives in this great American battle. In much the same way as Kim Phuc, Lincoln was bringing to the attention of the American mind that to truly honor those who died for the American cause, it was for the living to remain dedicated to the task remaining—"to do good things for the present and for the future to promote peace" (words of Kim Phuc). In Lincoln's words, "that this nation [and its ideals found in the Declaration of Independence and the Constitution], under God, ... shall not perish from the earth." President Lincoln and Kim Phuc were promoting the same concept just using different words—moving forward from a culture of war toward a civil and moral humanity based on forgiveness achieved through sacrifice.

For the readers of this book, please know that it was written to give numerous examples of sacrifice and heroism from many eras of American history. I have repeatedly emphasized throughout the pages of this work that to enumerate the endless acts of sacrifice in those critical times of American history would be an impossible task. It is the desire of this author, however, that if nothing else has been brought to the reader's attention, it is the hope that each reader has gained a new appreciation for the millions of sacrificial acts that have taken place in the annals of American history. Also the readers of this work should understand that many, if not most of the sacrifices throughout American history have been made not only for love of country but for fellow Americans (or other nationalities) as well, to save precious lives that were "in harm's way." And by the shear act of sacrificing to save lives, the act of sacrifice is also an act of true devotion to country and to God.

Jesus said, "Greater love has no one than this, that he lay down his life for his friends" (John 15:13, NIV). Jesus laid down his life and shed his blood as a sacrifice to cover the sins of every human being. Christ was the embodiment of the grace and forgiveness of God. Grace is unmerited favor. God's gift, as with any true gift reflecting love, is unmerited. It is up to every person individually to accept or reject God's gift of eternal life through the sacrifice of his Son, Jesus.

If you have never been to Gettysburg, you need to go. If you have never been to Flanders's Field in Belgium (it is actually American soil given to the United States as a memorial cemetery in 1937 for American soldiers who died in Meuse-Argonne offensive of 1918), you need to go. If you've never been to Pearl Harbor, you need to go. If you've never been to Shanksville, Pennsylvania, you need to go. If you've never been to Ground Zero in New York City, you need to go. If you've never been to the Vietnam War Memorial Wall in Washington, DC, you need to go. The number of names on that wall (all fifty-eight thousand) is staggering, and if you are a patriotic American, the experience is extremely humbling. The locations are almost endless. Realizing that everyone cannot physically go to these and thousands of other places where American sacrifices have occurred, everyone can go to these places of sacrifice in books or on the Internet. We all need to go because these and multiple other locations around this country and the world can remind us of our great heritage and the human sacrifice that was required to make our nation great and to provide the freedoms and security we all enjoy every day.

Take a few minutes and do an Internet query for American casualties in a given conflict. I'll make it easy for you—go to www. cnn.com/SPECIALS/war.casualties. Now peruse the American loss of life in the Iraq and Afghanistan campaigns over the past decade. This website makes lists of casualties much more personal because it lists personal facts as well as it shows pictures of the military personnel who gave their lives protecting freedom and the lives of innocent people in our most recent and continuing American conflict. But even after considering these sacrifices for freedom at home and around the globe, above all, we need to spiritually go to Jerusalem and to the foot of the cross where the greatest sacrifice and the greatest love ever known can be found. Be thankful! Do not forget the selfless acts of sacrifice made for our freedom—political and spiritual.

On September 11, 2011, many of us watched television news broadcasts of the ceremonies across America honoring the 2,977 humans who died a decade ago in the 9/11 attacks. From the ceremonies at Ground Zero, where all the names of those killed that fateful September day were read in about four hours, to Shanksville, where a group of American passengers overcame the terrorists forcing down United Airlines Flight 93 to crash before the terrorists could fulfill their murderous mission, to the Pentagon located in Arlington, Virginia, where American Airlines Flight 77 hijacked by terrorists killed 184 innocent victims by crashing that jetliner into the symbol of America's military power. Even the National Football League held moments of silence and patriotic pre-game presentations before every game remembering those who sacrificed so much on September 11.

Why go through all this ceremony? Why did it seem like everyone was waving an American flag? Why remember such horrible events? Why read the names of those who died? Why all the effort? Why all the tears? We do so not only because the lives of thousands of innocent people were snuffed out by an organized plot of murderous terrorists but because there were thousands of acts of heroism and sacrifice attempting to save the lives of fellow Americans, fellow human beings. Why? Because we need to remember. Remembering gives value to the very principles on which this nation was founded. Remember Lincoln's words: "government of the people, by the people, for the people, shall not perish from the earth." Lincoln was speaking of liberty and freedom, the very core of our nation's existence. But ultimately, we need to remember the acts of heroism and sacrifice because remembering gives value to life itself. In our remembrance, consider what General George S. Patton said, "It is foolish and wrong to mourn the men [and women] who died. Rather we should thank God that such men [and women] lived."

My prayer and purpose in writing this work is that all Americans will remember the sacrifices made for our nation. All sacrifice comes at a cost. But my prayer goes one step further. I pray that if God ever calls on me to sacrifice however great or small, even to the point of death like so many of those examples mentioned in this book, I will not shrink from the challenge. I hope that by reading the pages of this book, each reader will feel a sense of gratitude and a sense of duty to sacrifice for others ... family, friends, fellow Americans! After all, we do not live in fear, we live in freedom. We are Americans! And because we are Americans, we should not forget the sacrifices of those who not only fought to protect our freedom but more specifically, we should not forget those who gave their very lives fighting to protect those factions of humanity who were subjected to tyranny, inhumanity, and injustice.

In the same way, we should not forget the Savior who loved us all so much that he left his glory in heaven to willingly suffer and sacrifice his life to purchase our salvation. Those who are Christians know the spiritual gratitude and love one feels for the Lord Jesus Christ. The sacrifice of Jesus gave all who believe in his name the privilege of being a child of God with God's promise of an eternity spent with him in heaven. Without the sacrificial blood of Christ shed on that hill outside Jerusalem, no one could experience eternal life in the presence of God.

"Whoever believes in the Son of God accepts this testimony. Whoever does not believe, God has made him out to be a liar, because they have not believed the testimony God has given about his Son. And this is the testimony: God has given us eternal life, and this life is in His Son. Whoever has the Son has life; whoever does not have the Son of God does not have life" (1 John 5:10-12, NIV).

In *How Now Shall We Live?*, Colson asks that very question, "How now shall we live?" In our daily decisions that are lived out in our daily actions, what kind of world are we creating? What kind of legacy are we leaving to our children, grandchildren, friends and neighbors, our fellow Americans? My prayer is that we are living lives committed to God's truth according to his holy Word, serving others with love and sacrifice! *I believe that sacrifice is the essence of life itself.* Life continues only because sacrifices are made on many levels. But the greatest sacrifice in human history—the sacrifice of Jesus Christ on the cross at Calvary outside Jerusalem more than two thousand years ago—that singular sacrifice is essential for true life, which is eternal life with God in heaven.

Participant Guide

This participant guide is designed for individuals, adult Bible studies, or small groups as a supplement to the book *Sacrifice: The Essence of Life*. Although the study can be utilized and structured in a variety of ways to enhance individual and small-group study, it is designed to be implemented in a study of the concept of sacrifice over a period of eight to ten weeks. The material can be expanded for a longer period of study with in-depth Bible references, individual or group research, study, and discussion to meet the individual or groups' needs.

In *Sacrifice: The Essence of Life*, the author has attempted to give his readers a greater appreciation for the meaning of individual sacrifice. A fuller appreciation of the concept of sacrifice will lead the reader to a spirit of thankfulness and gratitude for what the past actions of others have done to solidify the ideals of freedom and liberty essential to the civil and spiritual freedoms that we enjoy but all too often take for granted. It will also lead to a deeper understanding of the sacrifice of Christ and how that single event not only fulfilled Old Testament prophecies but enriches our spiritual lives on a daily basis.

Using this participant guide for personal study or in small group settings:

This study guide is intended for individuals, adult Bible study or small groups. It is designed to deepen one's knowledge of the concept of sacrifice while weaving into the study themes of civil, political, patriotic, and spiritual issues with related discussions. The participant guide is designed to be utilized in a study series of no fewer than eight sessions but can be expanded comfortably to ten sessions or even more. Actually, the time frame of the study can be open ended, depending on the desire of the individual or group to research almost endless civil, political, patriotic, or Bible topics related to the concept of sacrifice.

It is strongly suggested that before each session, the individual or group:

- Pray. Ask God for guidance and wisdom in the study. How can the concepts and issues regarding sacrifice be applied on a personal or group level? What inspiration exists in the stories that can lead each person to a lifestyle of sacrifice? What lesson or lessons can be learned about God's expectations for personal sacrifice?

- Prepare. Each person should read the assigned chapter from *Sacrifice: The Essence of Life* prior to each meeting. The reading is essential so the entire group can be knowledgeable of the subject matter as well as being able to process the information from the book and benefit from the resulting group discussion. By way of the preparation, each person can make direct applications of the material to his or her life. Although specific research topics are suggested, the potential for further research on the subject of sacrifice is practically endless.

- Write. Write down not only answers to the questions posed in the participant's guide, but each person should write his or her own questions related to the topics presented. Do not be satisfied with the author's knowledge and questions. Make this your own research, and flavor your personal investigation with your own questions.

There is not a separate leader's guide with all the "right" answers in red ink. Adult Bible study and small-group leaders are actually "facilitators." As the group leader and facilitator, one should keep discussion moving, understanding that there are rarely any right or wrong answers (only in those situations where the Bible gives us God's specific "right answer"). Although discussion with debate will occur and should be encouraged, a ground rule for the group should be that respect for the opinions of others must be maintained at all times. No one should dominate the discussions, and everyone should be allowed a time to speak and express individual opinions. The group leader's job is to maintain an atmosphere of respect and at the same time move the group forward in the study and ultimately give God the glory for his wisdom as found in Scripture.

Finally, always search for the purpose that the author of *Sacrifice: The Essence of Life* had in mind. The purpose of the book is for the reader to not only learn of specific acts of sacrifice but to gain an appreciation for those acts, realizing always that sacrifices come at a price. In some cases the cost is extreme. Hopefully, the book brings each person to a point of reflection that makes the reader consider fundamental life values, fundamental life beliefs, and, ultimately, a fundamental and personal faith.

It's time to get started. Read the Introduction followed by Chapter One—"A Time Nearly Forgotten," do the necessary research, and come back next time ready to discuss it. I truly hope this study makes each and every person who reads *Sacrifice: The*

Essence of Life a better human being ... one who understands that sacrifice is an important and fundamental concept in our American culture, and as Christians, an idea that is the cornerstone of our actions and our faith.

Chapter 1

A Time Nearly Forgotten
(suggested time of study one to two weeks)

World War II hero Audie L. Murphy rose to national fame as the most decorated US combat soldier of World War II. Among his thirty-three awards and decorations was the Medal of Honor, the highest military award for bravery that can be given to any individual in the United States of America. He also received every decoration for valor that his country had to offer, some of them more than once, including five decorations by France and Belgium. Murphy became a legend within the Third Infantry Division. Audie Murphy was the most decorated American army infantryman in the Second World War.

Individual research:

Research the general causes of World War II. Find statistics about the war and the impact those statistics had on the United States (e.g., total number in uniform, total casualties—deaths and injured—POWs, change in industrial power, etc.).

Individually respond to the following questions with short answers and then discuss as a group. Ask additional questions related to the topic.

1. Regardless of age, most have some knowledge of World War II. Name one person you recall who was in any way, large or small, involved in World War II.

2. Name any family member, relative, or acquaintance who fought in World War II. Write any details you know about that person. How do you know these things? Have you ever spoken personally to this veteran? Did the person speak of World War II? If so, in what way?

3. The earth has been plagued since earliest times with wars between tribes, cultures, and nations. Human history chronicles hundreds of awful, gruesome, and blood-soaked wars. "Is war ever really necessary?" Why or why not?

4. After reading Chapter 1, "A Time Nearly Forgotten," do you think World War II was a necessary war for the United States? Why or why not?

5. Have you ever been to Pearl Harbor and the USS *Arizona* Memorial? What about other World War II sights— battlefields, concentration camps, or historically significant places? What impact did these locations have on you?

6. How would you define "sacrifice" after reading the various accounts described in Chapter 1?

7. Do you think your admiration and respect for a World War II veteran has changed at all after reading Chapter 1? Why or why not?

Read 1 Samuel 17 (David and Goliath) and answer the following:

1. With what people were the Israelites waging war?

2. Who was the "champion" of the enemy of Israel? Describe this "champion."

3. Why was there no Israeli soldier willing to fight "the giant"?

4. Why did David decide to fight "the giant"? What attribute did David possess that seemed to be lacking in all the others in Israel's army?
5. After slaying the giant, what did David do?
6. What, if anything, did David sacrifice in this well-known historical event?
7. How could a "warrior" like David, having fought and killed in the battles of Israel, be considered "a man after God's own heart"?

Final thoughts:

- Point #1—If you personally believe war is evil and one should never participate in a war, does that mean that, like millions of Jews in World War II, should one fall under the evil hand of tyranny (like a Hitler, Stalin, or any other despot in world history), one should (like those in concentration camps) simply accept a "sentence of death" without a fight? Why or why not?
- Point #2—If you believe there may be times when war is necessary (for the survival of a culture or belief system), are there any parameters on fighting and killing other human beings? In other words, how does one who believes that war may be necessary hold that position and yet believe in God's love for others and his commandment, "Thou shall not kill"?

Chapter 2

Another Time, Another Place
(suggested time of study one to two weeks)

Against the prospect of war between France and England, representatives from Maryland, New York, Pennsylvania, Massachusetts, Connecticut, Rhode Island, and New Hampshire met in Albany, New York, in 1754. Benjamin Franklin drew up a plan for common defense, which was signed by the members of the Albany Congress, although it was later rejected by the individual colonial legislatures. Though a failure, the plan was the first major attempt by the colonies toward a semblance of union and later became the basis for the First and Second Continental Congresses. Parts of Franklin's Albany Plan can be found in both the Articles of Confederation (1781) and US Constitution (1789). Benjamin Franklin, brilliant as he was as a statesman, knew the meaning of sacrifice and failure. He worked tirelessly toward the unification of the American colonies … even as early as his Albany Plan of 1754.

Individual research:

Research any single major event up to World War I (Revolutionary War, beginnings of the US government (1789), early presidents (Washington, Adams, Jefferson, Lincoln …), War of 1812, Mexican War, Civil War, Spanish-American War, World War I, etc., and give an example or two of sacrifices made at the time. This does not have to be extensive research—just familiarize yourself with a person or event and give an example of sacrifice.

Individually respond to the following questions with short answers and then discuss as a group. Ask additional questions related to the topic.

1. Everyone has heard of Benjamin Franklin. As was the case with other less famous people mentioned in Chapter 2, Franklin understood what it meant to "put it all on the line." Benjamin Franklin, like the fifty-six other signers of the Declaration of Independence, was actually signing his death warrant (had England won the war). In today's world, these acts of principle and support for belief systems are not readily reported but still do occur in other parts of the world. Why do we respect and admire such acts of principle and bravery?

2. George Washington, like Franklin, was a "larger than life" figure whose name is written in every American history book. He is often called the "father of our country." Do some research and make a short list of those things you think are important about George Washington. In your opinion, what was his most important historical contribution? In what ways did Washington sacrifice?

3. Had you heard the name Haym Salomon prior to reading *Sacrifice: The Essence of Life*? Why was Salomon's sacrifices important to the American Revolutionary cause? Although it is not an equal comparison with other historical times, how can we as Americans in the twenty-first century sacrifice for our nation? Why should we sacrifice, and why is it important?

4. The Civil War was the worst calamity in American history. More than six hundred thousand died in the four-year conflict. Were the sacrifices from that awful war worth it?

What did our country gain from the Civil War? What did it lose?

5. Do you agree or disagree with Dr. James Dunn's assessment of the sacrifice made by Clara Barton when he said after the Battle of Antietam, "In my feeble estimation, General George McClellan, with all his laurels, sinks into insignificance beside the true heroine of the age, the angel of the battlefield?" Why or why not?

6. Generally speaking, if people are asked to make a list of the ten most influential people in our country's (or the world's) history, the list would include more politicians and humanitarians than it would military personalities. If that is true, why is it that we tend to appreciate the sacrifices made on the battlefield more than the political sacrifices made in the halls of congress or the oval office? Is it morally acceptable to "appreciate" the battlefield sacrifices made by those who are "doing their duty"? Why or why not?

Final thoughts

- Point #1—Can we as Christians honor any actions of sacrifice related to war? Can we find any support from the words of Christ that would validate participation in war? Is there any scriptural support for personal participation in a nation's war efforts?

- Point #2—How do we as Christians rationalize any sacrifice other than sacrifices made for the betterment of others? Did Christ ever act in a violent or negative way toward anyone or any system devised by men? If you answered yes, when, where, and for what reason did Christ display such behavior?

Chapter 3

Unpopular Sacrifices

(suggested time of study one week)

The concept of sacrifice, especially sacrifice resulting in death or severe injury, is extremely difficult for many individuals to deal with psychologically. That is completely understandable considering the idea of sacrifice resulting in death or injury conjures up such bad images and unpleasant thoughts. In the cultural and historical mind of America, the Vietnam War conjures up just such images. Here are some facts about the war in Southeast Asia in the 1960s and early '70s:

- More than 2.7 million Americans served in the Vietnam War.
- 58,148 Americans were killed.
- 75,000 were severely disabled.
- 23,214 were 100 percent disabled.
- 5,283 lost limbs.
- Of those killed, 61 percent were younger than 21.
- 11,465 of those killed were younger than 20 years old.
- As of January 15, 2004, there are 1,875 Americans still unaccounted for from the Vietnam War.
- 97 percent of Vietnam veterans were honorably discharged.
- 74 percent say they would serve again, even knowing the outcome.
- Vietnam veterans are less likely to be in prison—only one-half of one percent of Vietnam veterans have been jailed for crimes.

- 85 percent of Vietnam veterans made successful transitions to civilian life.
- The average infantryman in the South Pacific during World War II saw about 40 days of combat in four years. The average infantryman in Vietnam saw about 240 days of combat in one year thanks to the mobility of troops provided by the helicopter.

Individual research:

Do a brief study about why the Vietnam War was so unpopular. The first sentence in Chapter 3 states, "No war should be popular." Knowing that should be true, what made Vietnam so different from previous wars? What role did the press, photojournalism, and videotape play in making this war different from all previous wars?

Individually respond to the following questions with short answers and then discuss as a group. Ask additional questions related to the topic.

1. What is your first impression reading the Vietnam War statistics above? Realizing it is only an opinion and there is no right or wrong answer, do you think from the United States' point of view, that the Vietnam War was worth it (politically, militarily, and monetarily)?
2. The first personal example given in Chapter 3 was the sacrifice made by Lieutenant Commander John McCain. Knowing what he went through and understanding the commander-in-chief responsibilities of the president, do you think military service is a valuable prerequisite to serving as president of the United States? Why or why not?

3. Twenty-four US presidents served in the military. Six were in the military but saw no action. Thirteen were not in the military. Can you list ten who served, two who saw no action, and four who were not in the military? (Go to http://www.heptune.com/preslist.html for the complete list.)

4. How do you interpret Jack Smith's comments in the final two pages of Chapter 3 regarding his service in Vietnam and the Battle of Ia Drang Valley? Do you believe, like him, that over time, "wounds heal"?

Final Thoughts:

• Point #1—Analyze the following Scriptures and discuss how, if at all, they relate to war: Romans 12:17-18; Romans 13:1-2; Exodus 20:13.

• Point #2—Consider the following Scripture: "For everything there is a season, and a time for every matter under heaven: a time for war, and a time for peace" (Ecclesiastes 3:1, 8, English Standard Version). There are those who consider themselves Christians (and no one is saying they are not Christians because of their views) who say Jesus was a pacifist (read Matthew 5:39 and 44). Read John's words in Revelation 19:11-21. John is certainly speaking of Christ and uses emphatic military terms such as "smite," "sharp sword," "armies of heaven," and "the kings of the earth with their armies mustered to do battle against the rider [Jesus] and his army." Is Jesus a pacifist? Is there a spiritual battle going on for the souls of men? Will Christ win such a spiritual battle by being pacifistic? Or is Jesus fighting a spiritual war that can only be won by defeating evil with God's righteousness?

Chapter 4

Everyday Heroes

(suggested time of study one to two weeks)

The Brooklyn Wall of Remembrance in New York stands as a beautiful tribute to those public servants who made the ultimate sacrifice on September 11, 2001. The memorial, comprised of three thirty by twelve foot walls of granite contain the engraved images of 346 firefighters, 37 Port Authority officers, 23 NYC police officers, 1 Fire Patrol first responder, and 1 K-9 rescue dog named Sirius. On the wall, their portraits form an inspiring and unforgettable testimony that reminds every American that these are real people behind the names and numbers who perished on 9/11. One-third of the responders who died that day either lived or worked in the Brooklyn borough where the Wall of Remembrance was erected. It has been so nobly stated, "Remembering is our responsibility, and learning from them is our honor."

Individual Research:

Of all the "first responders" who died on September 11, research only one and give a brief presentation of his or her life to the group. Include personal details such as age, background, education, family, hobbies, etc. In your presentation, give details that "personalize" this individual (because he or she was once an everyday American just like you and me). In your own words, try to describe the sacrifice this person made on 9/11.

Individually respond to the following questions with short answers and then discuss as a group. Ask additional questions related to the topic.

1. List other American historic events that could be compared to 9/11. What makes these events similar? Different?
2. After reading Chapter 4, list four or five personal characteristics that were shared in common by those "first responders" who lost their lives on 9/11.
3. Name any biblical events that could be viewed as similar to America's 9/11. Why are the biblical events similar?
4. In the aftermath of 9/11, America began a relentless pursuit of those terrorists responsible for the attacks. Comparatively, the Jew's Great Revolt (66-70 AD) was led by the Jewish Zealots, anti-Roman Jewish rebels who were active since the days of Jesus. The Zealots' most basic belief was that all means were justified to overthrow the tyranny and blasphemous teachings of Rome. Is America's pursuit of the terrorists, "by any and all means" and even into foreign nations which harbor the terrorists an acceptable policy? Is the hunting down and killing of terrorists like al-Qaeda's Osama bin Laden an acceptable act of the US government? Why or why not?
5. Matthew and Luke record Jesus' miracle when he healed the Roman centurion's servant. Obviously, to the eye of a first-century zealot, the Roman centurion who had charge of one hundred Roman soldiers was considered an enemy of Israel who was responsible for political and military oppression (and sometimes murder) in Israel. Jesus healed the centurion's servant. How can America's policies

of tracking and killing terrorists be consistent with Jesus' actions when he healed the servant of the centurion—an avowed enemy of Israel?

Final Thoughts:

- Point #1—US "special forces" such as Navy Seals or Delta Force perform a vital and oftentimes necessary function—special combat missions targeting counterterrorism around the world. In light of the recent mission in Pakistan to kill Osama bin Laden, what sacrifices do you think the members of these elite US military teams make for America (for us as American citizens)?
- Point #2—There are many "Wounded Warrior" programs under the auspices of the *Wounded Warrior Project*. Go online to www.woundedwarriorproject.org and see how combat stress recovery and physical health and wellness initiatives are benefiting our "wounded warriors" who have returned from Iraq and Afghanistan without limbs. It is worth your time (and your support) to see this program and the positive results it has brought to our wounded servicemen and servicewomen.

Chapter 5

A Different Form of Sacrifice
(suggested time of study one week)

People who do not know the Lord ask why in the world we waste our lives as missionaries. They forget that they too are expending their lives ... and when the bubble has burst, they will have nothing of eternal significance to show for the years they have wasted.

—Nate Saint

Individual Research:

Do a brief research project on Nate Saint and the Mission Aviation Fellowship. Nate is a modern-day example of a Christian martyr who gave his life in the mission fields of Central America (Ecuador). Result: the tribe that Nate and his fellow missionaries were trying to evangelize eventually were won to the Lord, including seven of the nine warriors who killed Nate and his four missionary friends in 1956.

Individually respond to the following questions with short answers and then discuss as a group. Ask additional questions related to the topic.

1. Read the commands of Christ to His disciples in Matthew 10 and 28. What is the difference between the two commands? How are they similar?
2. Are we, today's Christians (the Church of Christ), under the same command that Jesus gave His disciples in Matthew

28:19-20? If so, how are we supposed to follow Christ's command? Are we to do so individually or corporately (the church)?

3. Mission work costs money. Who pays the costs of missions? Who determines what missions are supported and how much should be appropriated and to which missions?

4. Why do you think all the apostles suffered a terrible martyr's death with the exception of John? Why do you think John was spared?

5. From the time of Christ (when the known world was ruled by Rome and Caesar worship as well as some other pagan gods) to the world today, where multiple "theisms" are practiced (even within the United States), the spread of the gospel of Christ has been risky and even life-threatening in many cultures. We are free to practice our beliefs and worship unmolested according to the laws of our land. How can we as free Americans gain a better understanding and appreciation for the difficulties and dangers faced by Christian missionaries around the world who evangelize daily in precarious and threatening conditions under regimes that are hostile to the Christian faith? How can we be supportive of these missionary heroes?

Final Thoughts:

- Point #1—Share your thoughts and personal experiences where you have served on a mission field or interacted personally with a missionary. How do the lives of "full-time" missionaries differ from your life on a daily basis? Should "mission work" (taking the gospel of Christ to foreign countries) be the primary focus of today's church? What about taking the gospel to non-Christians here in the states? Which mission focus is most important? Why?

- Point #2—The first ten amendments to the Constitution (The Bill of Rights) placed strict limitations on the power of government. Article I (the First Amendment) prohibits Congress from making any "law respecting an establishment of religion, or prohibiting the free exercise thereof ..." The basis of our government is individual liberty within a system of governance whose power comes from the people. Do we, as American Christians, take this freedom for granted? Is there any danger that this most basic freedom (religion) could be taken from us? If you think there is a danger, how do you think such a grievous violation of the Bill of Rights could occur (the real question is, "Can you name other societies where a once held right of religious worship was taken from the people by a despotic government?")?

Chapters 6 and 7 combined

Closer to Home (Chapter 6)
(suggested time of study 1 week)

Individual Research:

The only exercise relating to Chapter 6 is for each person to briefly share his or her recollections of early childhood through the teen years. How did those years impact the "rest of your life"? Also, make a short list of the ways your parents sacrificed for you (and your brothers and/or sisters).

Sacrifices in Early Civilizations (Chapter 7)

"In war, diplomacy, inventions, and art, the Hebrews made a little splash in the large stream of human history. In religion and ethics, however, their contribution to the world civilization was tremendous. Out of their experience grew three great religions: Judaism, Christianity, and Islam."—*A History of the Hebrews*

Individual Research:

Using online resources or other resources at your disposal, draw a simple timeline of the Hebrews from Abraham to Jesus to the founding of the nation-state of Israel in 1947. Do not make this complicated—just make a simple timeline with major events in Hebrew history. This will give everyone a better perspective on history and each person will definitely learn something new.

Individually respond to the following questions with short answers and then discuss as a group. Ask additional questions related to the topic.

1. Refer to Genesis 10 to find the lineage of Abraham dating back to Shem, a son of Noah. The Hebrew people descended from Shem although it is actually with Abraham that the story of the Hebrews begins. How did God intervene in Abram's life, and what kind of covenant did God make with Abram (Genesis 15)? What country ("land") was given Abram (now Abraham) and to his descendants?

2. Describe the "test" God put to Abraham in Genesis 22. What historical foreshadowing do you see in Genesis 22:2-15?

3. Where did the Twelve Tribes of Israel originate (see Genesis 48 and 49)? Under what circumstances did the Israelites (descendents of Abraham and Jacob) find their way to Egypt (Exodus 1)? Approximately how long was the Hebrew captivity in Egypt?

4. Give a description of the arc of the covenant (Exodus 25 and 37). What was its purpose? What was the purpose of the tabernacle (Exodus 25-29)?

5. The root of the Hebrew word for altar means to "slay or sacrifice." The Latin word "alta" means "high"—a high place for sacrifice. Why do you think many ancient cultures and religions used animal or even human sacrifices? Why did the Hebrews use blood sacrifice or atonement (see Leviticus 17:11)?

Final Thoughts:

- Point #1—Study Isaiah 53 and list the references to the "suffering servant" and sacrifices mentioned there. Do a brief search of Old Testament Scripture that predicts the coming of a Messiah.

- Point #2—In your own words, explain why as a Christian we should believe that the Jewish tabernacle and Temple worship system was the "one and only" forerunner to the messianic sacrifice found in Christ? What would the Jewish sacrificial system have meant if Christ had not been a Jew, proved his deity via miracles, and eventually his death on the cross and then his resurrection from the dead?

Chapter 8

The Ultimate Sacrifice

(suggested time of study 1 week)

But they cried out, "Take him away, take him away,
crucify him." "Shall I crucify your king?" "We have no
king but Caesar," the chief priests answered. Finally
Pilate handed him over to them to be crucified. So
the soldiers took charge of Jesus. Carrying his own
cross, he went out to a place of the Skull (which in
Aramaic is called Golgotha). Here they crucified
him, and with him two others—one on each side
and Jesus in the middle.

—John 19:15-18

Individual Research:

Pick up a copy of Mel Gibson's *The Passion of the Christ*. Watch
the scenes showing the scourging of Jesus and His crucifixion, as
difficult as that might be. Write down your feelings. Write down
how the scenes affect you physically and mentally. Also write down
specifically what Jesus means to you. Although you certainly don't
have to share these most personal and intimate feelings, if you desire
you may share them with the group. If you are unable to find a copy
of *The Passion of the Christ*, find a reliable written explanation of the
affects of scourging and crucifixion, read them, and then write your
feelings as specified above.

Individually respond to the following questions with short answers and then discuss as a group. Ask additional questions related to the topic.

1. Christ's trials, both civil and religious, are prime examples of what can happen under any government that is a dictatorship. The trials of Jesus were a sham, no different from the trials held in Nazi Germany, fascist Italy, Imperial Japan, Communist Soviet Union, or a multitude of other countries under the thumb of tyranny and dictatorship. The bottom line for Jesus was that he was a "trouble maker" for the Jewish religious leaders and His popularity was getting out of control. He had to be stopped. For what specific reasons did the Jews and Romans prosecute Jesus? Review and make a list from Chapter 8 of the various "illegalisms" that transpired during the trials of Jesus.

2. What historical sources outside the words of the New Testament validate the life, teachings, and claims of Jesus? According to Miami University's noted historian Edwin Yamauchi, what specific things can we know from reliable historical sources outside the New Testament writings?

3. There are many theories that claim that Jesus really did not die on the cross. Examples are: (1) stolen body theory—followers of Jesus stole the body from the tomb; (2) swoon theory—proposed that Jesus actually fainted and was not really dead when taken down from the cross; (3) drugged body theory—that Jesus was actually drugged and thought dead; (4) twin theory—some advocated Jesus had a twin brother who was actually crucified in the place of Jesus; (5) vision theory—in despair the apostles literally saw visions of

Jesus; (6) spiritual resurrection theory—some believe Jesus actually was resurrected spiritually but not in physical body form—and the list goes on and on. How do we know that without question Jesus did die a physical death?

4. What is the unexplainable mystery about the death of Jesus, his substitutional death for the sins of man, his "becoming sin" (or a "sin offering"), and God the Father's holy righteousness that cannot look upon "unrighteousness" (sin)? At least try to explain this most interesting mystery.

5. What was the purpose of the veil (curtain) in the Holy of Holies? Why was it torn in two when Jesus died on the cross (Hebrews 10:19-22)?

6. How did Jesus sacrifice for you? Reference Philippians 2:5-7 and Hebrews 9:24-26.

Final Thoughts:

- Point #1—How is Jesus, his crucifixion, and the shedding of his blood the symbolic representation of the tabernacle, Temple, Holy of Holies and the "mercy seat"? How does the blood of Jesus "fulfill the law" and cover (atone for) our sins and satisfy God's righteous judgment against sin? See Isaiah 53.

- Point #2—The temptations of this world can easily lead men and women away from a loving, personal relationship with God through Jesus Christ. Jesus said, "I have told you these things that you may have peace. In this world you will have tribulation, but be of good cheer for I have overcome the world" (John 16:32-33). Can a person have possessions (money, land, homes, "things") and still have eternal life through Jesus? If so, how?

Conclusion and Final Thoughts

(suggested time for conclusion one week)

After reading and discussing *Sacrifice: The Essence of Life*, does the word "sacrifice" now have a deeper meaning when you hear it? Will you ever be able to use the word sacrifice in any context without giving full attention to the details and significance of the event? The word sacrifice must remain a part of our vocabulary. My hope is that by digesting the concepts contained in *Sacrifice: The Essence of Life*, each reader will view with awe and reverence the concept and definition of the word sacrifice.

We as followers of Christ have an awesome responsibility. First Peter 2:21 says, "To this you were called, because Christ suffered for you, leaving you an example, that you should follow in his steps." We must emulate Christ in word and deed. If we truly claim him as our Savior and Lord, we know that he sacrificed beyond our comprehension, leaving his glory in heaven and his perfect relationship with his Father in heaven. Jesus sacrificed so we might be saved to live with him eternally in heaven. Jesus paid the cost to redeem us unto his Father.

So "How Now Shall We Live?" What kind of spiritual legacy will we leave our children, grandchildren, friends and neighbors, our fellow Americans, the world?

Yes, I believe *sacrifice is the essence of life!* I will leave you with one final set of questions. Answer them individually and then use the group format to discuss your answers. Thank you for reading, researching, discussing, and giving yourself to this study. My prayer is that you were blessed by it. My prayer is that you were changed by it!

- **Who was Jesus?**

- **What did Jesus do for you?**

- **What did Jesus give up for you?**

- **Why did Jesus do it?**

- **How did Jesus endure it?**

- **What does Jesus' sacrifice mean to you?**

- **How will you respond to Jesus?**

About the Author

John Abell is a native of Indiana. Born in 1949, John grew up in Greenwood, a small community south of Indianapolis. Greenwood was like Mayberry, a small town where everybody knew everybody. It was a great place to grow up and be a kid. There were Little League games, homecomings, corner drug stores with fountain Cokes and milkshakes, a boys' club, several churches, small businesses, a public library, a small theater, and a drive-in. John attended Greenwood Community Schools, getting a sound education at the hands of caring and dedicated teachers. He loved sports and participated in cross-country, basketball, and baseball in high school.

After graduating high school, John attended Butler University in Indianapolis, majoring in history and political science. John graduated from Butler in 1972 with a bachelor of arts degree in a pre-law curriculum with a license to teach social studies. John began his thirty-six-year profession in secondary education when he took his first teaching and coaching position at Carmel High School, Carmel, Indiana, in the fall of 1972.

John married his wife, Gloria, also a graduate of Greenwood High School, just before he started his teaching career. Gloria graduated the following year from the University of Indianapolis as a licensed elementary school teacher. She was an elementary school teacher for thirty years, also in the Carmel School system.

John continued his education, receiving his MS and EdS degrees. After ten years in the classroom, John began a twenty-six year career in high school administration, where he held positions of dean, administrative assistant, assistant principal, and principal at Carmel High School. In 2005, John was selected the "Indiana Assistant Principal of the Year" by his peers in the Indiana Association of School Principals.

John and Gloria have two grown children, Kelli and Ryan, as well as six grandchildren. John has, in the past seven years, participated in mission trips with FAME (Fellowship of Associates of Medical Evangelism) and LIA (Life in Abundance International) in Honduras, Ethiopia, and Kenya. Now retired, John and Gloria enjoy family, friends, church activities, and travel.

References

Introduction

1. www.americanrhetoric.com/speeches/ronaldreaganatimeforchoosing.

Chapter 1

1. Marines World War II. www.MarinesWWII.com
2. Department of the Navy, Naval Historical Center Homepage, www.history.navy.mil/faqs/faq11-1.htm.
3. Battle of Okinawa Statistics, www.jahitchcock.com/okibattle.html.
4. Laura, Hillenbrand. *Unbroken* (New York: Random House, 2010), 43.
5. Ibid.
6. Ibid, 88.
7. History of the Second World War, Part 68, Marshall Cavendish Promotions Limited, 1975.
8. Ibid.
9. Jewish Virtual Library, www.jewishvirtuallibrary.org/jsource/biography/Bonhoefer.html.
10. German Culture, germanculture.com.ua/library/weekly/oscar_schindler.html.
11. Naval History and Heritage, www.history.navy.mil

12. Military.com Unit Pages, Histories for the Eighty-Second Airborne Division, www.military.com/HomePage/UnitPage.

13. US History.com, "Bataan Death March," www.u-s-history.com/pages/h1737.html.

14. Naval History and Heritage. www.history.navy.mil.

15. Hillenbrand, Laura. *Unbroken* (New York: Random House, 2010), 35.

16. America in WWII http://www.americainwwii.com/stories/luckylouie.html.

17. Ibid.

18. Ibid.

19. Hillenbrand, Laura. *Unbroken*, (New York: Random House, 2010), 93.

20. _____. *Unbroken*, (New York: Random House, 2010), 103.

21. _____. *Unbroken*, (New York: Random House, 2010), 80.

22. www.news.ninemsn.com.au/8427036/battle-of-sundra-strait.

23. USS Indianapolis: www.ussindianapolis.org.

24. Military Times Hall of Valor: www.militarytimes.com.

Chapter 2

1. National Parks Service, Department of the Interior, American Revolution: Haym Salomon www.nps.gov/revwar/about_the_revolution/haym_salomom.

2. David McCullough. *1776* (New York: Simon and Schuster, 2005), 247.

3. "The American Drummer Boy." http://www.americandrummerboy.com/

American_Drummer_Boy/The_Real_Drummer_Boys/
Entries/2008/10/17_William_Horsfall.html.

4. Randall, J. G. and David Donald. *The Civil War and Reconstruction* (DC Heath and Company, 1969), 531.

5. The American Civil War, www.americancivilwar.com

6. Randall, J. G. and David Donald. *The Civil War and Reconstruction,* (DC Heath and Company, 1969), 231.

7. www.military.com.

8. Ibid.

9. Ibid.

10. Congressional Medal of Honor: www.cmohs.com.

11. Barron, Elwyn A. *Deeds of Heroism and Bravery: The Book of Heroes and Personal Daring,* (New York: Harper & Brothers Publishers, 1920), 13.

12. America's Story. www.americaslibrary.gov

13. *Webster's New World Dictionary,* The World Publishing Company, 1964.

Chapter 3

1. McCain, John. *Faith of My Fathers,* (New York: Random House, 1999), 188-89.

2. _____. *Faith of My Fathers,* (New York: Random House, 1999), 221.

3. _____. *Faith of My Fathers,* (New York: Random House, 1999), 289.

4. www.Edwikipedia.org.

5. Army/military: www.army.mil/medalofhonor.

6. http://www.mishalov.com/death_ia_drang_valley.html.

7. Ibid.

8. Aviation Hall of Fame: http://www. aviationhalloffamewisconsin.com/inductees/sijan.htm

9. Congressional Medal of Honor: www.cmohs.org.

10. Ibid.

11. http://www.mishalov.com/death_ia_drang_valley.html.

12. McCleery, Bill. "A Patient Hero," *The Indianapolis Star,* April 5, 2012.

13. Website: www.civilwarhome.com/warstats

Chapter 4

1. Jennings, Rob. *The Daily Record,* http://charlieblack.net/tributes/rescorla.html#rescorla_jennings.

2. Tapsbugler: http://tapsbugler.com/from-vietnam-to-the-world-trade-center/.

3. NYPD Angels: http://www.nypdangels.com/nypd/smith.htm.

4. Officer Down Memorial Page: http://www.odmp.org/officer/15818-police-officer-moira-smith.

5. http://www.cnn.com/SPECIALS/2002/america.remembers/stories/heroes/welles.html.

6. http://www.unitedheroes.com/Thomas-Burnett.html.

7. http://www.unitedheroes.com/Todd-Beamer.html.

8. Positivity: Remembering 9/11's Heroes. http://www.bizzyblog.com/2010/09/15/positivity-remembering-911s-heroes-leonard-hatton-fbi/.

9. Officer Down Memorial Page. http://www.odmp.org/officer/16195-fire-marshal-ronald-p-bucca.

10. http://www.newsday.com/news/printedition/longisland/ny-liange042809601aug04.

11. The *New York Times,* November 6, 2001.

12. "America Remembers," ABC News, September 11, 2011.

13. http://en.wikipedia.org/wiki/September_11_attacks.

14. www.wthr.com/story/13910211/officer-moore-passes-away.

15. http://articles.cnn.com/2001-09-11/us/bush.speech. text_1_attacks-deadly-terrorist-acts-despicable-acts?_s=PM:US.

16. The *Indianapolis Star*, May 2, 2011, A1 & A8.

17. The *Indianapolis Star*, May 3, 2011, A9.

18. About US Military: http://usmilitary.about.com/cs/navy/a/navyseal.htm.

19. http://articles.latimes.com/2011/aug/06/world/la-fg-afghanistan-chopper-20110807.

20. http://www.washingtonpost.com/blogs/checkpoint-washington/post/marine-cpl-dakota-meyer-receives-medal-of-honor/2011/09/15/gIQACqAKVK_blog.html.

21. http://www.washingtonpost.com/world/national-security/former-marine-to-receive-medal-of-honor/2011/08/12/gIQASpYxBJ_story.html.

22. http://projects.washingtonpost.com/fallen/iraq/.

Chapter 5

1. Fox, John. *Fox's Book of Martyrs* (Zondervan Publishing House, 1967), 2.

2. Hurriyet Daily News: www.hurriyetdailynews.com, Dogan News Agency, July 7, 2011.

3. http://www.online-bible.org.uk/apostles/apostle-matthew.

4. Fox, John. *Fox's Book of Martyrs* (Zondervan Publishing House, 1967), 3.

5. Ibid.

6. Ibid.

7. Ibid.
8. Biblepath. "Answers from the Bible" :http://www.biblepath.com/peter.html
9. Ibid.
10. Ibid.
11. Fox, John. *Fox's Book of Martyrs,* Zondervan Publishing House, 1967, 4.
12. Christian History: http://www.christianitytoday.com.
13. Bible Gateway: www.biblegateway.com/resources/commentaries. Acts 14, *Matthew Henry's Concise Commentaries on the Bible.*
14. Fox, John. *Fox's Book of Martyrs* (Zondervan Publishing House, 1967), 4.
15. Ibid.
16. www.britannica.com/EBchecked/topic/54362.
17. Fox, John. *Fox's Book of Martyrs* (Zondervan Publishing House, 1967), 4.
18. Victor Shepherd: www.victorshepherd.on.ca/Sermons/Luke.htm
19. www.britannica.com/EBchecked/topic/30740.
20. http://en.wikipedia.org/wiki/Barnabas#Martyrdom.
21. http://en.wikipedia.org/wiki/John_the_Apostle.
22. Fox, John. *Fox's Book of Martyrs* (Zondervan Publishing House, 1967), 5.
23. www.theblaze.com/stories/2013/01/07/iranian-pastor-youcef-nadarkhani-released-again-following-christmas-day-arrest.
24. *60 Minutes,* 10/9/2011 telecast. CBS News television.
25. www.nydailynews.com/news/world/2011/10/09.

26. http://www.wnd.com/?pageId=61272.

27. www.chinaaid.org.

28. http://www.chinaaid.org/2011/10/congressional-report-on-china-500.html.

Chapter 6

1. "The Resolution," as seen in the movie *Courageous:* http://www.courageousresolutioncertificate.com/resolution-certificate-courageous-movie.html.

2. www.worldvision.ca, "The Hard Facts on Poverty."

3. "The world hunger problem: Facts, figures and statistics." http://library.thinkquest.org/C002291/high/present/stats.htm.

Chapter 7

1. http://en.wikipedia.org/wiki/Sacrifice.

2. http://en.wikipedia.org/wiki/Western_Orisha.

3. "A history of sacrifice cannibalism." http://www.hyperhistory.net/apwh/essays/cot/t0w13cannibalism.htm.

4. Becoming Jewish: www.becomingjewish.org/theology/sacrifices_and_offerings.html.

5. http://en.wikipedia.org/wiki/Temple_in_Jerusalem

6. The Tabernacle Place. http://www.the-tabernacle-place.com/tabernacle_articles/tabernacle_ark_of_the_covenant.aspx

7. Ibid.

8. Messianic Jewish Life: www.TheMessiah.org.

9. Ibid.

10. Bible Study Tools: http://www.biblestudytools.com.

11. Messianic Jewish Life: www.TheMessiah.org.

Chapter 8

1. Insight for Living: www.insight.org/library/articles/pastoral-resources/courtroom-fiasco.
2. Ibid.
3. Ibid.
4. Ibid.
5. Ibid.
6. Blue Letter Bible. "Medical Aspects of the Crucifixion of Jesus Christ." http://www.blueletterbible.org/commentaries/comm_view.cfm?AuthorID=3&contentID=3129&commInfo=8&topic=Crucifixion.
7. Strobel, Lee. *The Case for Christ* (Zondervan, 1998), 87.
8. Ibid.
9. Ibid.
10. Ibid.
11. Ibid.
12. Ibid., 223.
13. Fountain of the Spring: http://www.fountainofthespring.org.
14. The Tabernacle Place: http://www.the-tabernacle-place.com/tabernacle_articles/tabernacle_holy_of_holies.aspx.
15. "Jesus Messiah," Chris Tomlin. 2008 worshiptogether.com Songs (admin. by EMI CMG Publishing)/Six Steps Music (admin. by EMI CMG Publishing/Vamos Publishing (admin. by EMI CMG Publishing) (ASCAP)/Alletrop Music (BMI).
16. Miller, Rhea F. "I'd Rather Have Jesus," Chancel Music, Inc., 1966.

Conclusion

1. Canadian Centers for Teaching Peace: http://www.peace.ca/kimstory.htm.
2. http://en.wikipedia.org/wiki/Phan_Thi_Kim_Phuc.
3. Colson, Charles. *How Now Shall We Live?* (Tyndale House Publishers, 1999), 482-3
4. Ibid, 485-6.
5. Ibid, 486.

CPSIA information can be obtained at www.ICGtesting.com
Printed in the USA
LVOW121027310513

336234LV00003B/15/P